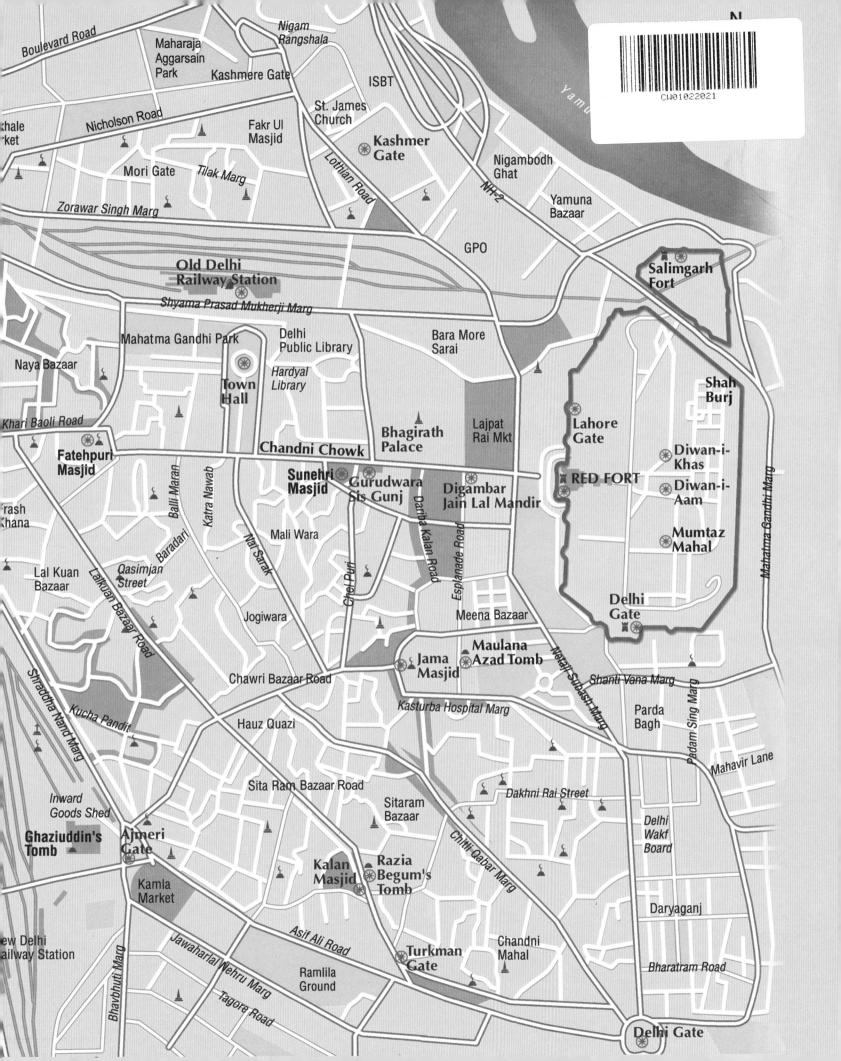

DELHI

The Emperor's City

ISBN: 81-7436-240-1

Text and Photos: Vijay Goel
e-mail: vgoel@sansad.nic.in

© Vijay Goel

Roli & Janssen BV 2003
Published in India by
Roli Books in arrangement
with Roli & Janssen BV
M-75 Greater Kailash-II (Market)
New Delhi 110 048, India.
Phone: (011) 29212271, 29212782
Fax: (011) 29217185
Email: roli@vsnl.com
Website: rolibooks.com

Scanned and Processed by
Radiant Graphics, New Delhi

Printed and bound at Singapore

DELHI

The Emperor's City

Rediscovering Chandni Chowk and its Environs

Vijay Goel

Lustre Press
Roli Books

Dedicated to

Shri Atal Bihari Vajpayee

Who has and will continue to inspire me

Contents

The arches, courtyard and the young ladies in traditional dress peeping from the balcony were typical of life in havelis. (Picture from Haveli Ballimaran)

East side of royal palaces in the Red Fort. Watercolour on paper, Company School, Delhi: c.1836.

Preface

My fondness for monuments, forts, and old havelis that epitomize the rich cultural heritage of our nation has been the guiding force behind this book.

I am a *Dilliwalla* (native of Delhi), born and brought up here. I have grown up around the Walled City variously known as Shahjahanabad, *Purani Dilli* (Old Delhi), *Purana Shahar* (Old City). To us *Dilliwalas* it has always been *Dilli*, the capital city of the mighty Mughal Dynasty. New Delhi is a town the British built to showcase their hold over India. *Dilli* and New Delhi are two different worlds, two different cultures. New Delhi has peaceful coexistence. *Dilli* has the *Ganga-Jamuni tehzeeb* (the best of Islamic and Hindu etiquette). My father had an office in Khari Baoli and I too have my paper business headquartered in Chawri Bazaar. Delhi is where my roots are.

While visiting the forts and havelis of Jodhpur and Jaisalmer in Rajasthan, I went to see *Patwon ki Haveli* which, I must admit, was in a rather deplorable condition. I immediately found myself asking who the Member of Parliament of the area was, who was responsible for such gross neglect? As a corollary, I also ended up thinking of the deteriorating situation of Chandni Chowk, and the fact that I represented the area in Parliament inspired me to do something.

It shall be my endeavour through this book to highlight that there is still much to be cherished in Chandni Chowk.

Perhaps the main reason behind the steady deterioration of this erstwhile imperial city is that its charming havelis and other edifices are private properties and have been drastically altered over time, with unscrupulous builders playing a pivotal role in converting traditional houses into markets. Compounding the problem is the sheer indifference of civic agencies and local bodies that have led to a virtual collapse of the system.

The Archaeological Survey of India is a case in point. Instead of adding more monuments to its list of 'protected monuments', its efforts have often been insufficient in protecting those that are already on the list. While NGOs and individuals form a separate group, it would not be unfair to

Facing page: The imposing doorway of a haveli in Churiwalan depicts the ornate architecture of Shahjahanabad. The door has a hunting scene carved on it.

The grand Jama Masjid built by Shahjahan is used as a venue for political rallies.

say that this multiplicity of agencies is leading to utter chaos.

I remember the time I undertook the task of organizing the first cultural festival called *Chaudvin ka Chand* in Chandni Chowk. It attracted more than half a million people in a single day, and it wasn't a one-day festival. It was the outcome of the efforts of my friends, workers and the residents of Delhi that helped a glorious past come alive. It entailed pulling down hundreds of ugly signboards, giving the city a uniform whitewash, painting the streets with colour, removing garbage from the surroundings, restoring the havelis and other landmarks. The Herculean task would have been impossible to accomplish but for the active participation of all.

I was moved to tears when people kissed my hands and congratulated me for this huge success in showcasing glimpses of the culture of the Old City. The overwhelming success of this festival— that too thrice—together with the restoration of Mirza Ghalib's haveli was enough to reconfirm my faith in this couplet of his.

One desert will not stop my ardent quest, it is but a bubble on a billow's crest which aids the tide.

— Mirza Ghalib

My well-wishers warned me of the hazards of such a venture, stating reasons why the thing was bound never to take off. I was reminded of the time a few years ago when I started a campaign to ban lottery all over India. I had heard similar prophesies and yet the campaign was a huge success. I knew then I was going to be successful this time too.

The task of restoring this city to its past splendour is very dear to my heart. I propose that Chandni Chowk be declared a 'Heritage City' and be allocated special funds and a separate board for looking after its day-to-day functioning. Life is to be evaluated using practical parameters. I have decided to make Chandni Chowk a pedestrian-friendly city, free of all major problems. These include issues as diverse as traffic congestion and lack of heritage awareness to tangled electrical and phone cables. Steps have been taken to revive a declining food culture and keep alive the unique art and craft traditions, and I request all of you to participate in and contribute to this cause.

This book concentrates on several aspects of Chandni Chowk's rich culture. Addresses of monuments have been provided so that people can visit them. The book endeavours to help future generations understand and appreciate our magnificent past, and is also for visitors who seek to explore the city.

I am grateful to the generosity of friends and colleagues who shared their time and knowledge and have helped with the compilation of this book. I am especially indebted to **Mr Sunil Kumar Ahuja,** my photographer and to **Vikas Bhardwaj** for his contribution towards research and documentation. I am also thankful to my wife **Preeti Goel** for her continuing support and encouragement. Without their unfailing commitment to my beliefs, this book would never have been possible.

Courtesy: Hindustan Times

Chaudvin ka Chand Utsav lights up Chandni Chowk.

Bazaar Matiya Mahal (mud-coloured palace) where Shahjahan once lived while the city was being constructed.

Introduction

Delhi is a city that has seen both glory and destruction in its long and chequered history. It has been plundered, defaced and ruined time and again only to spring from its very ashes to become the capital of powerful dynasties. Temperamental and proud, this eternal city allowed only the most powerful to rule it. In a wry vein this Rajasthani couplet aptly sums *Dilli: 'Dilli Raand Dogali, Aatan No Jaato Karey; Nar Dekhe Naato Karey Bhoganiyan Ne bhog Lee.* (*Dilli* is a fickle one she shoos away fasinated suitors. Only those who come up to her exacting standards enjoy her favours.)' Fortunately, the resilient and enduring culture and heritage has withstood the test of time and the city continues to live. No city reflects the endless drama of change better.

Delhi has a hoary past dating back to the times of the *Mahabharata* when it was known as 'Indraprastha' (it is said to have had its beginnings in 1450 B.C.), the current habitation has seen the emergence of at least ten cities through the thousand years it has been in existence. None of the cities is so redolently Mughal, so typically an archetype of its most powerful and famous ruling dynasty than *Dilli*.

The heart of Delhi can be found in Old Delhi, three hundred and fifty years old, yet strong and beating. Its many-branched arteries are narrow with age, its veins jostle for space, and its lifeblood is bound to get clotted at some places at any time (a first time visitor may just have many an anxious moment). But, elsewhere, perhaps inside an old vacant building it can relax, and flow in peace and silence. In documenting *Dilli*, this book, like a pulse, throbs to all its different heartbeats.

The city originated, it is said, when the fort at Agra faced agonizing heat, coupled with insufficient accommodation and space for Shahjahan's lavish lifestyle and his grand ceremonial processions. The emperor chose a site south of Salimgarh after consulting Hindu astrologers and Muslim *hakims* (physicians).

The city of Shahjahanabad (the Abode of Shahjahan), interestingly, bears a woman's stamp. It was Jahan Ara, the favourite daughter of Shahjahan, who laid the foundation of the city around 1639. According to the *Shahjahanamah* and the *Mirat-e-Aftab Nama* (books on the life and times of the emperor), backed by inscriptions found on the *Khwabgah* (the sleeping quarters), the city's foundation was laid on 12th Zilhajjah 1048 A.H. in the eleventh year of the emperor's reign. Construction began on 29 April 1639. According to historian John. F. Richards, '*The Fort and its buildings cost nearly Rs. six million. Finally, on the auspicious day of 8 April 1648, Shahjahan formally entered Shahjahanabad. Revelry and royal largesse followed for days as nobles, scholars and dignitaries assembled under a great canopy of embroidered velvet in the Fort's Diwan-i-Aam or Hall of Public Audience.*'

'*Kaun Jaye Zauq par Dilli ki galiyan chhod kar* (How can anyone bear to go away leaving the lanes of Delhi behind?)', wrote Sheikh Muhammad Ibrahim Zauq, court poet of the last Mughal Emperor Bahadur Shah Zafar. At Chandni Chowk or The Moonlit Square, which is the most famous area of Shahjahanabad, that verse can easily be a refrain.

Chandni Chowk, once the biggest commercial centre of the East, is a world in itself. Noisy, cluttered, yet magical. Its bazaars, *galis* (lanes), *mohallas* (localities), *katras* (fort markets), and *kuchas* (streets) are anchored in a bygone era.

Chandni Chowk was originally built as an open octagonal space located outside Begum Bagh. A branch of the Yamuna canal passed down the middle of the street and formed a pool that reflected the moon, and so the square came to be named Chandni Chowk.

The Chowk developed from the Lahore Gate of the Red Fort to the Fatehpuri Mosque and was divided into four parts. The area from Lahore

Elderly men recreate an old-world ambience; the traditional carpet, the hookah and the manner of restful hospitality speak of an age of leisure, conviviality and high culture. (Picture from Haveli Ballimaran)

Gate to Dariba Kalan defined the first part and was known as Urdu Bazaar. It has a notable temple, the Digambar Jain Lal Mandir, which was known as the Urdu Mandir during the staunchly orthodox Mughal Aurangzeb's reign. Legend has it that when Aurangzeb once tried to prevent devotees from offering prayers in the temple, the bells within the temple started ringing on their own and Aurangzeb was forced to open the temple.

The second part, the Kotwali, was the seat of the *Qazi* (the Muslim judge who dispensed judgement according to Muslim laws). Today the site lies adjacent to the Sunehri Masjid or Golden Mosque near the North Brook Fountain. The third part is the Asharfi Bazaar. It extended from the Kotwali to the Town Hall, and was also named Faiz Bazaar after a canal, the Faiz Nahar, which flowed through the Chowk. The fourth and final part extended up to the Fatehpuri Masjid.

The Red Fort and Jama Masjid were the starting point for two straight thoroughfares that framed the city. From Lahore Gate ran a broad avenue with a covered arcade—designed and paid for by Jahan Ara—that housed over fifteen hundred shops. This bazaar is today known as the Chatta Bazaar.

The remainder of Shahjahanabad took shape within the city walls with its havelis, mansions, mosques, temples, sikh shrines and the gardens of the nobility. The walled and guarded establishments of these grandees included private living quarters for the nobles and their harem,

CHANDNI CHOWK: LORE & LEGENDS

Chandni Chowk is the smallest parliamentary constituency of the world's largest democracy. In its many lanes, *galis*, *katras* and *kuchas*, we find remnants of India's past, the roots of India's culture and the essence of what is known as the *Ganga-Jamuni tehzeeb*. Chandni Chowk, as it had existed a couple of hundred years ago, was a street made of bazaars with a row of banyan trees down the centre, with the silver ribbon of the flowing canal flanked by a wide platform where people sat and conversed. Horse-driven carriages, palanquins and sometimes elephants passed through the street.

Courtesy:Victoria and Albert Museum, London

1 A marketplace for princesses

Mughal Emperor Shahjahan's daughters were extremely fond of jewellery. The emperor commissioned a whole market, **Dariba Kalan**, for them. The shops in Dariba Kalan displayed a wide array of pearls and other precious stones. It also became immensely famous for its *halwais* (sweetmeat sellers), who offered such rich delicacies as *Kadhai Doodh* or sweetened milk.

2 Ghalib's jail

The place where the **Kotwali** once existed is now an extension of the Gurudwara Sis Ganj, built in the memory of Guru Teg Bahadur who was martyred in 1675. Among its former inmates was the renowned Urdu poet Mirza Ghalib who, interestingly, was arrested for gambling by Lakhani Rajput Kunwar Wazir but was set free on bail and his sentence suspended. Purani Kotwali also witnessed the outrages committed by the British. On the *chabutra* (platform) opposite, the bodies of Mirza Mughal Khizr Sultan (Bahadur Shah Zafar's son) and Mirza Abubaqr (grandson) lay exposed for four days. On a later date, it saw the execution of twenty-one princes, nawabs and other dignitaries after the British recaptured Delhi. Maulana Fakhr-ud-din, buried near the mosque of Khwaja Qutb-ud-din Bakhtiyar Kaki in Mehrauli, had his residence behind the Kotwali.

3 Here money was king

Kucha Mahajani owes its name to *mahajans* (the moneylenders) who inhabited it. The main source of income for these moneylenders was usury—such was their power and wealth that even the Mughal princes were often indebted to them.

4 Booklovers' haunt

Nai Sarak (New Street) has always been a place for *purani* or old books. It has traditionally seen students exchange books sometimes for other books or money. The place comes alive every day when thousands of books line the street and draw bibliophiles from all over Delhi.

5 Freedom fighters threw a bomb

Katra Dhuliyan witnessed a heroic chapter in our struggle for independence. Revolutionaries threw a bomb on Lord Hardinge's procession from the upper floor of a building here. The Viceroy escaped unhurt, but the man who held the Viceregal umbrella died. The revolutionaries Avadh Bihari, Amir Chand, and Balmukund were later sentenced to death and hanged.

6 The indigo connection

Katra Neel, as the name itself suggests, housed the famous indigo sellers, though this is not its sole claim to fame. The place was a seat of unrest during the 1857 War of Indepedence. Also, many people laid down their lives here during the course of the Quit India Movement (1942-1945).

7 A sweeper's fortune

Behind the peculiar name, **Katra Asharfi**, lies an interesting story. A rich *Seth* (merchant) while serving meals to his daughter's *baratis* (the bridegroom's guests) placed an *asharfi* (gold coin) next to the *thalis* (plate) of the guests as the custom called for. The *baratis* neither liked the way in which the coins were given nor were they happy with a single coin each. They left in disgust without the coins, and the following morning, a sweeperwoman found a fortune on the streets. Hence the name.

8 A poet's kucha

The famous poet Daagh was born in Kucha Ustad Daagh, though he was brought up in the grand Lal Qila (Red Fort). He learnt under the court poet, Zauq, who was equally famous. In 1857, Daagh left for Rampur and found his place in the Nawab's court. In 1888, the Nawab of Hyderabad acknowledged Daagh as his teacher.

9 Ghalib's Jaan

Off Ballimaran lies a lane, Qasim Jaan, where the famous poet Mirza Asadullah Khan Ghalib (1797-1869) lived. Most of his matchless poetry and ghazals (poetry set to semi-classical music) were composed here.

10 Wrestlers' arena

This housed the numerous akharas (wrestling rings) where wrestlers were trained and pitted against each other that brought fame to Gali Kaccha Bagh. Choti Bench (the lower courts) were also located in this part of Shahjahanabad.

11 The Sabeel

The Sabeel, originally known as Islamic Sabeel, is said to have existed from the time of the glorious uprising of 1857, though the structure was made permanent only in 1885. It was here that water was offered to passers-by, travellers and probably to the wounded during the revolt.

12 Poor man's street

If ever a street has soaked sweat, it must be the Gali Ghantewali. Quite obviously its inhabitants were the poor: the thelewallas (cart-pullers) and jhalliwalas (porters) who traded their labour for pennies. Their presence was necessitated by the fact that Chandni Chowk was also an important business centre and merchants needed people to cart their merchandise.

13 Gali Parathewali

Certain families that settled here specialized in making parathas with different vegetable stuffings. So it became famous for its delectable parathas. The space is still renowned for its traditional cuisine. The photograph shows Pandit Jawahar Lal Nehru at the Gali with Vijaylaxmi Pandit, Indira Gandhi and Babu Jagjivan Ram. Till date Shri Atal Bihari Vajpayee relishes the dishes served here.

Earlier, traders used to sit on the floor on *gaddis* (floor cushions) and conduct business, in what was known as the *gaddi* style.

their officers and clerks, their slaves, servants and soldiers—the largest amongst which may have housed over two thousand persons. Around these sites lay clustered the dwellings of hundreds of urban citizens who were dependent upon the patronage of traders and others amongst the business class. Every day, public rituals of Islamic secular and religious life were enacted in the bazaars, *hamams* (baths), *sarais* (public houses), *baghs* (gardens) and masjids or mosques. Every day the nobility held court in their mansions throughout the city, imitating rituals of the imperial court but on a lesser scale.

Shahjahanabad had magnificent gardens commissioned by members of the royal family. It was filled with superb mosques easily identified by their glittering domes, and the residences of proud Mughals, now converted into havelis. It had some fine streets, with innumerable small ones joining them. Dubbed the Rome of Asia, it was a splendid urban creation that, unfortunately, has not been maintained. Apart from the shortage of funds required to maintain the havelis, the pace and the trends of modern life have forced residents to change their lifestyle and divest themselves of their tradition and culture.

The scent of the flower, the smoke of the candle, the lament of aching hearts, whoever left your salon, left distraught.

— Mirza Ghalib.

Ghalib could easily have had Chandni Chowk in mind. The Chowk is at par with the world's best-known squares such as Trafalgar Square in London, Piazza Novena in Spain, Tiananmen Square in China, New York's Times Square and the Red Square in Moscow. Even amongst these, it is the only place in the world that has monuments dedicated to different faiths on one road: Digambar Jain Lal Mandir, Gauri-Shankar Mandir, Arya Samaj Diwan Hall, the Central Baptist Church, Gurudwara Sis Ganj, Sunehri Masjid and the Fatehpuri Masjid. However, Chandni Chowk was, and is, primarily a commercial centre. Its shops were and are abundantly stocked with exotic wares and trinkets that would enchant any lady, and rouse the muse within any virtuoso. Fruits, sweetmeats and dry fruits from Bukhara, Isfahan, Baghdad, Kabul, Istanbul and Tabrez came to the bazaar. Some of that continues to hold true of today as well.

Before *swadeshi* (a term that connotes economic self-reliance) became a strategy to win emancipation from the British, the Chowk housed imported goods: woollens and textiles from Glasgow and Manchester, watches from Switzerland, perfumes from France, shoes from Italy, scissors from Germany, needles from England, and crystal from Belgium. Even today the streets of Chandni Chowk are abundantly stocked—with shops full of fabrics, gold and silver jewellery, embroidered and leather goods, carpets and enamels. Also for food enthusiasts— gastronomic delights around every corner. But entry into the fabled area is hard because pollution and noise can confound and disorient the shopper.

The author of an eighteenth-century geographical compendium had this to say about Shahjahanabad: 'Delhi was always the Dar-al-Mulk [Seat of the Empire] of the great Sultans.'

Today, too, Old Delhi is a vibrant hub not only for commerce but also for various religious centres of great sanctity that continue to exist side by side. One easily finds tombs and graves of dozens of holy men who are revered within its walls.

Magnificent Mansions

Home to a plethora of opulent mansions, Shahjahanabad was indeed a visual delight. The high-walled mansions with gardens and fountains

In the bullion trade market at Kucha Mahajani a man takes a break on silver bricks.

were for *amirs* (nobles) and princes. These mansions or havelis had beautiful facades, often with exquisite inlay work in semiprecious stones. A French traveller wrote: 'There are many mansions of the nobles, which one can compare to small towns and in which goods and bazaars of the nobles exist.' The lower-ranking nobles and rich merchants had smaller houses constructed of baked earthern tile and limestone or brick. Ordinary merchants often lived in the quarters behind their shops. Craftsmen, servants and small traders lived in mud huts that lay scattered all around the city.

As one moved from the centre towards the interior, a marked difference could be made out in the architectural styles of the city. The larger mansions had a thick wall of stone surrounding them, and they housed soldiers, guards, drummers, trumpeters and musicians. An area around the forecourt was also designated for keeping horses and elephants or bullock carts—now used by some havelis as a garage. Apart from the main quarters of the mansion, there were apartments for clerks and servants, storerooms for grain and armouries. The facilities could sustain a community within the walls in times of need, such as a siege.

Light and air came in through slatted lattices that deflected the direct glare of the Indian sun, while arched niches with intricate designs acted as lamp and candle stands. Fountains spouted cool water in the central pool. Sadly, today not a trickle of water is visible in several dilapidated mansions. True, some havelis in Shahjahanabad still have traces of glittering glass and polished marble floors. But as commercial interests take over, for most havelis the countdown has begun.

Time has taken its toll on so much here. The *lakhori* brick houses (made of small bricks used during the later Mughal period) are still there, and many havelis still boast of fine carvings and designs on their facades and interiors, yet the present hardly indicates the past. With the past rapidly changing into myth, what is left is just a small glimpse into a grandeur once visible everywhere.

> Not all, just few have manifested themselves in the form of rare blooms. Myriad are the glories that remain entombed.
>
> —Mirza Ghalib

Imperial Society

Imperial society in seventeenth-century India was divided according to assigned duties. *Ahadis* or single troopers, numbering 7,000 in 1648, according to the *Badshahnama*, served as cavalrymen, as part of the emperor's private bodyguard, or as officials in the administration that managed the imperial household. Then came the *Walashahis* or attendants that included military men who served the king. A number of rules governed court protocol and etiquette.

Shahjahanabads' society comprised a mingling of international as well as national strains, sheltering diaspora from all over the world. By the early 1730s, the city had absorbed various elements from neighbouring regions, and it

Vendor sitting in front of the beautifully carved haveli 2559 in Dharampura.

One of the surviving cinema halls in the Walled City. The others have been converted into unauthorized markets.

housed not only the ruling elite and other officials of the state but also a large number of people from different communities: *Kayasths* (court scribes), *Sarrafs* (jewellers), *Mahajans* (moneylenders), brokers, *Pandits* (Brahmins), *Jats* (agriculturists), craftsmen, peasants, shopkeepers, poets, artists and mendicants. Professionals such as doctors, teachers, lawyers, high officials and domestic soldiers were also an important and integral part of society.

The Kashmiri Pandits had begun migrating to the plains from the time of Sikander Lodi. The Mughals adopted a conscious policy of integrating them into society and by the beginning of the eighteenth century, the core group of Kashmiri Pandits in Delhi had indeed become a sizeable community—engaged as poets, lawyers, scholars and *diwans* (ministers). *Khattris* (traders) were also employed by the state and by the nobility after the sixteenth century. They were in government services and also participated in trade and commerce in large numbers, though their business establishments were mostly family-run. Over time, they were able to garner an enormous amount of wealth and were owners of a substantial number of large, beautiful havelis.

Their havelis dominated areas such as Dariba Kalan, Maliwara, Roshanpura, Katra Neel, Kucha Ghasiram and Kashmere Gate.

The Jains too were an integral part of Shahjahanabad and contributed towards the economy of the region as jewellers, moneylenders and heads of craft guilds. They built rich and ornate temples individually or through their *panchayats* (units of self governance).

Educated people and professionals had been in demand since the time of Shahjahan. The Walled City boasted of some of the best professionals. In the field of medicine, Hakim Baqa who lived near Hauz Qazi was very famous. Hakim Sanaullah Khan, Hakim Namdar Khan, and Hakim Kamdar Khan were also well-known names. There were specialists residing in various *kuchas* and *katras*. Hakim Ajit Singh lived in Kucha Maliwara and Hakim Mian Khan in Muhalla Ballimaran. Later, Hakim Ajmal Khan became an important figure: he institutionalized Unani medicine in the early twentieth century. His family lived in a haveli, Sharif Manzil, located in Ballimaran.

During the Mughal period, the quarters of the Walled City were loosely divided on the basis of different guilds. Localities inhabited on the basis of specialized professions were Katra Neel, parts of Lal Kuan, Bazaar Sita Ram, Roshan Pura and Tiraha Bairam Khan. Several Pandits resided in Muhalla Bulbul-i-Khana, Chatta Lal Miyan and Pahari Bhojala.

The size of a *kucha, gali* or *katra* varied. Traditionally, the term *katra* stood for an enclosed market and *kuncha* (also, *kucha*) referred to a street with a dead-end. There could be *kuchas* in *katras* or *katras* in *kuchas*. Most of them took a prefix or suffix that pointed to the specialized product sold or manufactured there. Katra Neel, for example, has the Hindi word *neel* as a suffix; *neel* means blue and is even today used to denote indigo, the whitening agent. Katra Neel, therefore, was a locality famous for indigo manufacturers and traders. In much the same manner, Gali Samosa was known for its samosas, the famous Indian snack: a fried vegetable patty, triangular in shape, that is stuffed with spicy potatoes and peas. Churiwalan was famous for its bangle sellers and manufacturers.

A *katra* or *kucha* could also be named after the most important person of the area; or a noble's haveli that had been converted into a *kucha* or *katra*; or after some principal landmark in the area like Kucha Lal Kuan and Kucha Pahari. A *katra* could be named after the community living in the area such as Jatwara, Mochion Ki Gali, Suiwalan and Gali Pattewalan.

Though these *kuchas* and *katras* are well known, Chandni Chowk is famous for its colourful bazaars that are popular for their special products. Chawri Bazaar is still famous for copper and brass utensils, paper products and printing items. Charkhewalan used to be a production centre for the manufacture of catherine wheels. The Sirkiwalan Bazaar at Hauz Qazi was famous for *sirki* or reed grass used for thatching. Bazaar Dariba Kalan is known for the polishing of

Delicious parathas being prepared in Parathewali Gali.

precious stones and for engraving and embellishing marble with stone chips of various colours or mirrors with ivory or jewels. It is also a place that those with a sweet tooth love to visit. *Halwais* (confectionary chefs) are at work all hours of the day here making various desserts also known as *mithai*; their jalebis are a delicious treat and worth their weight in gold.

Kinari Bazaar has the most wonderful glittering shops in the whole of Old Delhi. It is the centre of commerce that provides goods for the colourful and ornate Indian wedding ceremony. The shops are full of gold-lamé turbans for grooms, garlands strung with currency notes and

huge rosettes. It is not only traditional Hindu costumes that are available here. Brides and their families—irrespective of whether they are Hindus, Sikhs, Muslims or Christians—visit the bazaar to buy finery for their individual wedding requirements. During festival seasons such as Dussehra, shops start stocking bows, arrows, maces, and colourful dresses.

A not-to-be-missed place is the Ghantewala Sweet Shop (literally, The Bell Ringer's Sweet Shop). Today, Haldiram is also another sweet shop here. The name of Ghantewala seems a fragment from Mughal times: whenever great processions passed through Chandni Chowk, the

A typical shop in Kinari Bazaar, festooned with glittering trinkets, is a fascinating window into a sparkling world.

royal elephants would refuse to move till they were given some sweets.

Delicacies like *sohan halwa* (gram flour biscuits cooked in ghee), *kaju ki burfi* (cashewnut fudge), *laddoos* (small balls made of flour, ghee and sugar), *imarti* (lentil roundels dipped in sugar syrup), and *sohan papri* (a flaky, layered sweet made of sugar, ghee and flour) are readily available. Most are served with silver foil on top, known as *vark*.

Bazaar Matiya Mahal literally means the Bazaar of the Mud-Coloured Palace. The palace, no longer exists, and what is left are shops that sell delicious Mughlai food and Urdu books. The shops themselves differ from those in other areas of Chandni Chowk in terms of the clothing material and bangles they display. These reflect the characteristic ethos of the region. Several restaurants line the Bazaar's street, the most famous being Karim's. Its delectable kebabs are irresistible and popular all over Delhi.

Khari Baoli (The Well of Brackish Water) is one of the busiest and most aromatic streets! The dry fruit and spice shops found there are a gourmet's delight, heaped with *badam* (almonds),

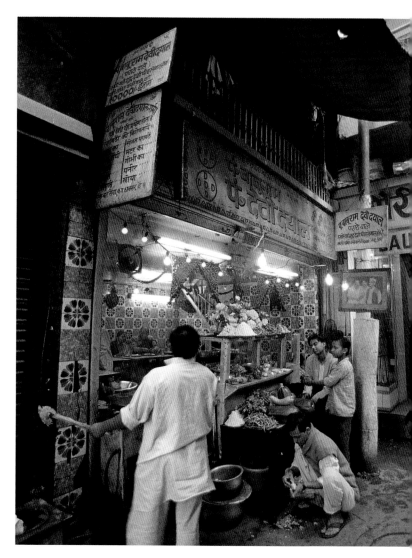

Food being prepared is a colourful feast for the eyes under the bright lights of a local eatery.

kajoo (cashewnuts), *nariyal* (coconuts), *jaifel* (nutmegs), *munakka* (sultanas), *moongphali* (pcanuts), *akhrot* (walnuts), betelnuts, *kishmish* (raisins) and *anjeer* (dried figs). The area is also famous for its *thandai* (a refreshing milk based cold drink topped with rose petals).

Among the twentieth-century additions to the Chowk is Nai Sarak. It was built over a hundred years ago after the Mutiny (First War of

A fascinating window display of traditional handcrafted jewellery.

Independence) of 1857 and houses the largest book market in India. The Lajpat Rai Market, named after the great freedom fighter and built in 1950 is a thriving centre for trade in electronic goods.

The multiple strains gathered in Shahjahanabad contribute towards its varied cultural fare while its inhabitants exhibit exquisite tastes. The residents' lifestyles add to the city's rich ambience. The Walled City was, once upon a time, an unmatched miniature that showcased Delhi's immense grandeur and grace. It was a typical oriental city of vibrant charm and beauty. Today it has become a ghetto beset with problems.

It is in a state of disorder and chaos that requires a Herculean corrective effort.

The city's decline is traced to the invasion of Nadir Shah in 1739, also seen as the beginning of the decline of the Mughal Empire. Nadir Shah ordered a massacre on 11 March 1739 that left 30,000 of the citizens dead. He returned to Persia with arms and magnificent treasures that included the Koh-i-Noor diamond and the Peacock Throne. The fabulous dream that was Delhi had begun to fray at the edges.

Courtesy: Victoria and Albert Museum, London.

Chandni Chowk epitomizes universal brotherhood. This photograph shows Sikh holy men leading a religious procession through the Chowk.

A *Ramleela* performance adds to the gaiety of the Dussehra festival.

Shahjahan's City Today

The mystic poet Kabir wrote a famous verse about the potter's wheel. 'The potter is the maker who fashions the clay of man into shape.'

The past provides an elegant background in the form of Jama Masjid for young cricket enthusiasts relaxing after play.

Since the Raj, playing carrom-board has been a popular pastime in Old Delhi.

CHAPTER 1

The deep moat surrounding the Red Fort is one of the features responsible for the low battlements.

History
IN
Stone

E ven though most of the grand structures of Shahjahanabad are now in ruins, history unfolds itself here building by building, site by site. The city used to boast of several palace complexes. Today, they serve as examples of architectural splendour and are a pointer to how outside influences and indigenous features can be blended in perfect harmony. An important feature of Shahjahanabad's architectural heritage is its style of building and design: it is in consonance with the way of life of its residents. Thus, the city's structures also depict its cultural links. India's most formidable feat in historical

architecture, however, had its origins in an emperor's wish.

'It first occurred to the omniscient mind [a reference to Shahjahan; exaggerated honorifics to monarchs were the norm] *that he should select on the banks of the river [Yamuna] some pleasant site, distinguished by its genial climate, where he might found a splendid fort and delightful edifices, agreeable to the prompting of his generous heart, through which streams of water should be made to flow and the terraces of which should overlook the river.'* Thus wrote Mohammed Tahir Inayat Khan in the *Shahjahanama*.

Such a vision obviously required that something as glorious as the Red Fort, be built: an edifice that represented the pinnacle of Mughal palace fort building and symbolized political and economic power. Architectural historian Percy Brown judged the Red Fort in 1942 as *'the last and finest of those great citadels representative of the Muslim power in India, the culmination of the experience in building such imperial retreats which had been developing for several centuries'*. Indeed, the Red Fort symbolizes the apex of Mughal cultural refinement—easily one of the most sophisticated theatres built in the world for the unfolding dramas of the Mughal court.

The Red Fort, that took nine years and three months to build, was completed on the 24th of Rabi'u-l-awwala in the twenty-first reigning year of Emperor Shahjahan corresponding to 1657-58. The cost was an astronomical six million rupees. It seemed that with its construction one of the verses of Amir Khusro on Delhi had been proved prophetic:

'Ghar Firdaus bar Roo-i-Zameen Ast; Hamin Asto, Hamin Asto, Hamin Ast. (If there is paradise on earth – It is here, it is here, it is here.)'

Ustads Hamid and Ahmed, master architects of Shahjahan's time, were employed to construct the fort. Arched screens, marble inlay work, pietra dura representations, *jharokhas* (windows), marble lattices and the fine craftsmanship on the windows add to the beauty of the painted mansions and residences that comprise the Red Fort. The Yamuna flowing by enhanced it to perfection. This effect is, of course, lost today. But in 1784 the river used to flow so close to the fort that a prince who was anxious about losing his royal life, jumped from a Red Fort tower into the river, swam across it and fled to Lucknow!

Built of local stone and in a simple design, Shahjahanabad had fourteen gates. The *khirkis* or wicket-gates built for residents of different

mohallas or localities were also fourteen in number.

When the British came to the city they also added their buildings, and erected monuments worth cherishing and preserving. Shahajahanabad's culture thus reflected the true and diverse spirit of humanity in a blend of lifestyles. Be it the simple designs executed in Delhi quartzite stone or the colonnaded arches of the Red Fort, they represented the Mughal ruler's grand architectural style.

Yet, the critical need for conservation crossed the thoughts of neither the builders nor of those who came after them. The physical face of Shahjahanabad, its ethos and culture have suffered as a result. The silent fort buildings, havelis, religious edifices and historical structures are fighting a losing battle. But despite the ravages of time and human action, many irrevocable, the extraordinary achievements of Indian architecture remain visible in the remnants that can be seen today. James Ferguson, writing in 1910 in *History of Indian and Eastern Architecture* pointed to the gravity of the situation:

'The palace at Delhi is, or rather was, the most magnificent palace in the east, perhaps in the world. The gems of the palace [remain], it is true, but without the courts and corridors connecting them they lose all their meaning and more than half their beauty. Situated in the middle of a British barrack yard, they look like precious stones torn from their settings in some exquisite piece of an oriental jeweller's work and set at random in a bed of the commonest plaster.'

If this was the state of affairs in 1910 one can imagine the state today. But Shahjahanabad is unmistakably rich in history. It was in Chandni Chowk that Dara Shikoh (Shahjahan's favourite son and Aurangzeb's rival) was executed in 1659 and his body paraded in the street as a warning to local supporters by Aurangzeb. It was into this city that revolutionaries marched in May 1857 during the Mutiny. The next year Emperor Bahadur Shah II (1837-58) was deposed, and the Mughal Empire fell, giving way to the British Raj.

Shahjahanabad's walls are monuments to history. Its buildings have charm and are a tribute to the Walled City that it was and is, despite the ravages of time, a symbol of power and prestige.

Delhi Gate

LOCATION: Daryaganj, at the intersection of Asaf Ali Road and Netaji Subash Marg.

SIGNIFICANCE: Built in the 1650s, this is one of the four surviving Gates of the original fourteen gateways of Shahjahanabad. It is called the Delhi Gate because it opened towards the old cities of Delhi during the time of Emperor Shahjahan.

EXPLICATION: Constructed with local stone and in a simple design, this domed roof gateway has pointed arched openings with bastions at each end, while mouldings and battlements complement its attractive dimensions.

Gallows Bastion

LOCATION: The NCC office compound, near the Traffic Court, Kashmere Gate.

SIGNIFICANCE: Built in the 1640s, the site is located on the city wall over a circular bastion that was made of stone. The diameter of the hole at the upper level is about 1.2 metres.

EXPLICATION: Innumerable freedom fighters were hung to death at the gallows here by the colonial state. The relatives collected the bodies of those who were executed from a lower level on the other side of the well.

Kashmere Gate

LOCATION: Near the Inter-State Bus Terminal (ISBT).

SIGNIFICANCE: Built in the 1650s during Shahjahan's reign. This is one of the four surviving gates of the original fourteen gateways of Shahjahanabad. The road through it eventually led to Kashmir, hence the name. During the Great Indian Mutiny of 1857, when the situation was extremely grave, it was via the Kashmere Gate that British forces entered Delhi at dawn on 14 September 1857.

EXPLICATION: This Gate has two arched openings with compartments on either side, while a domed roof and battlements form the seminal constituents of the edifice.

A memorial for British soldiers

On a stone tablet at the foot of the central wall between the two arched openings stands a memorial. General Lord Napier of Magdala, Commander-in-Chief of British India in 1876, built it as a tribute to the soldiers who sacrificed their lives during the Mutiny. Houses with features similar to the houses found in the Himalayan regions can be seen in the area surrounding Kashmere Gate.

Skinner's Family Cemetery

LOCATION: St. James' Church Compound, Kashmere Gate.

SIGNIFICANCE: Apart from its immense architectural significance, this nineteenth-century cemetery is the burial ground of James Skinner, the Englishman who built St. James' Church in 1836.

EXPLICATION: The tombstones, several of which are rather well preserved, are made of white marble. The fine artistic and aesthetic sense is appreciable.

Grave tales

Near this cemetery lie two important graves—those of William Fraser and Thomas Metcalfe. William Fraser, Resident of Delhi, was the first Commissioner and Agent to the Governor General at Delhi in 1832. The same year the Resident was re-designated Civil Commissioner and Agent to the Governor General at Delhi. Fraser lived at Hindu Rao's mansion on the Ridge, before he was murdered in 1835. Thomas Metcalfe (full name Thomas Theophilius Metcalfe) was the younger brother of Charles Metcalfe. He arrived in Delhi in 1823 and succeeded David Ochterlony as the British Resident.

Mirza Ghalib ki Haveli

LOCATION: 2298, Gali Qasim Jaan, Ballimaran, Chandni Chowk.

SIGNIFICANCE: Mirza Ghalib, the great nineteenth-century poet shifted to this haveli in 1860. He continued to live there till his death on 9 February 1869.

EXPLICATION: Originally known as Karora Wali Haveli, the entrance from Gali Qasim Jaan has a slightly projected central arch which leads to a gallery representing the works of Mirza Ghalib. The central arch is flanked by two arches and staircases on either side. The haveli, now a memorial, depicts the life history of Mirza Ghalib through portraits, manuscripts and exhibits displayed in showcases.

Early years of Ghalib

Ghalib was married at the age of thirteen to Umrao Begum, daughter of Illahi Baksh Khan, younger brother of Ahmed Baksh Khan, Nawab of Ferozpur Jhirka Loharu. He shifted to Delhi within a year or two of his marriage and stayed with his father-in-law, before moving out and living in different rented houses in Ballimaran.

Diwan-i-Aam

LOCATION: To the east of the Naubat Khana, Red Fort.

SIGNIFICANCE: Built between 1639 and 1648 the Diwan-i-Aam and its courtyard were officially marked off into several divisions for the durbars of the emperor.

EXPLICATION: Emperor Shahjahan used to hold durbars or courts for the general public in this hall. The court has splendid sandstone columns with cusped arches and a marble pavilion; it was decorated with gold stucco work. The interior of the hall is three bay deep. It is 24.4-metres long and 12.2-metres wide and stands on a 1.2-metre plinth. It has fluted columns and a curved Bengal roof.

The seat of the shadow of god

Shahjahan used to spend about two hours a day, between eight and ten in the morning, at the hall. There he worked on matters of governance and received petitions. The marble canopied throne on which he sat was known as Nishan-i-Zill-i-Illahi, The Seat of the Shadow of God. The inlaid panels behind the canopy were made in Florence, but Indian craftsmen executed all the floral inlay work.

The colonnaded arches of the Diwan-i-Aam flanking the marble throne of Shahjahan.

Artist's rendition of Lahore Gate (Red Fort: c. 1639-48)
Facing page: Lahore Gate in the west side of the Red Fort.

Lahore Gate

LOCATION: Facing Chandni Chowk Bazaar.

SIGNIFICANCE: Also known as Victoria Gate, it stands today as the most important and most frequented gate of Red Fort. The Prime Minister addresses the nation on Independence Day from here.

EXPLICATION: It consists of three storeys and while the upper rooms now afford accommodation to the officers of the Fort, the lower ones serve as guardrooms. The centre of the facade above the gate has a row of dwarf *chattris* (umbrellas), each topped by a small marble dome.

Diwan-i-Khas

LOCATION: Red Fort.

SIGNIFICANCE: Built between 1639 and 1648, with two courtyards, one in front and one on the west, enclosed by arcaded colonnades. Also known as the Shahi Mahal or the Royal Palace where the *umras* and nobles of high rank waited on the emperor when he granted private audience. Over the corner arches of the north and south walls, under the cornice, is written a much-quoted verse: 'If there is paradise on the earth— it is this, it is this, it is this'. A fitting tribute to the splendours of Shahjahanabad.

EXPLICATION: The hall is 27.4-metres long, 20.4-metres wide, standing on a 1.4-metre-high plinth. The pietra dura work on the lower level of the arch piers is magnificent. A marble water channel, the Nahr-i-Bahisht, runs through the centre of the hall. The Diwan-i-Khas was the spot from where the 1857 sepoys proclaimed Bahadur Shah Zafar the Emperor in May. The British deposed him and seven months later, he was tried at the same spot for the 1857 Mutiny and exiled.

The Peacock Throne

The Peacock Throne, or the Takht-i-Taus, was about six feet long and four feet wide, studded with gems and designed like a peacock. The canopy was like a fanned-out tail. Its estimated cost was Rs 10 billion in the 1630s. A marble dais is said to have supported the throne which was looted by Nadir Shah in 1739.

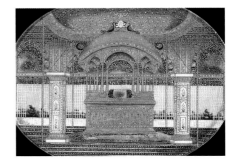

Company Bagh

LOCATION: North of the Town Hall.

SIGNIFICANCE: Originally a garden built by Jahan Ara Begum in the seventeenth century, the British redesigned it as the Company Bagh in the nineteenth century.

EXPLICATION: Palm trees of the Colonial era and the royal fencing still add glamour to the park. A statue of the Father of the Nation, Mahatma Gandhi, has been installed in the centre of the Bagh. The Delhi canal, known as Faiz Nahar, or more commonly as the Nahar-i-Sadat Khan, ran through it.

An exclusive club

The park acted as an outdoor club for Delhi's intelligentsia, doctors, lawyers, judges, teachers and administrators who worked in Chandni Chowk. The green lung provides a much-needed breathing space today. This is one of the few untarnished spaces of the old Chandni Chowk, that was once a cluster of gardens, mansions and fountains.

Tomb of Ghaziuddin

LOCATION: Anglo-Arabic Public School, Ajmeri Gate.

SIGNIFICANCE: Ghaziuddin, the son of Nizam-ul-Mulk, founder of the Nizam Dynasty of Hyderabad, was one of the leading nobles in the court of Aurangzeb and Farrukhsiyar. During his lifetime, he built a mausoleum and a madrasa in the early eighteenth century.

EXPLICATION: The inner enclosure contains three graves, the central resting place is that of Ghaziuddin Khan. Four coloured sandstone *jaalis* (pierced screen work) carved with floral designs adorn the tomb. The marble screens topped by balustrades are a good example of *jaali* work.

Aurangzeb's commander

It was common for Mughal noblemen to want their tombs to be an integral part of an educational centre since Islam gave literacy a high place. Ghaziuddin was a successful commander in Aurangzeb's army. In 1689 he fell seriously ill and it left him blind. Yet, Aurangzeb continued to solicit his advice.

Turkman Gate

LOCATION: Asaf Ali Road.

SIGNIFICANCE: Built in 1658, during Shahjahan's time, it is named after Shah Turkman. Turkman Gate is another of the four surviving gateways of Shahjahanabad.

EXPLICATION: The Gate is a two-bay deep structure with a flat roof in the first bay and a domed second bay. It is flanked by flower medallions in the spandrels of the arches, battlements, cusped arches and semi-octagonal, double-storeyed turrets.

The saint of wilderness

Shah Turkman was a holy man of great repute. He died on 19 February 1240. His real name was Shams-ul-Arifin, but he was also called Biyabani because he lived in the wilderness (biyaban).

Ajmeri Gate

LOCATION: Ajmeri Gate Chowk, Kamla Market.

SIGNIFICANCE: Built during 1644-1649 this is yet another of the four surviving main gates of Shahjahanabad.

EXPLICATION: The Gate is a single-arched structure with semi-octagonal turrets on the outside. The gateway, that was recently repaired, is decorated with niches and *kanguras* (decorative motifs on parapets). A fountain has been added and the Gate is surrounded by a beautiful park.

Old Secretariat

LOCATION: Shamnath Marg, Civil Lines.

SIGNIFICANCE: Calcutta (now Kolkata), not Delhi, was the capital of India until 1911. The Legislative Council used to meet at the Government House in Kolkata. Following the decision to transfer the capital to Delhi, E. Montague Thomas, an Englishman, designed the Old Secretariat building that was completed in 1912.

EXPLICATION: The Old Secretariat is a handsome building with a long front line and two lateral structures. The portion facing Alipur Road (Shamnath Marg) curves gracefully in the centre like a half moon. A large veranda with square archways and rounded pillars runs in front of the office.

Venue for debates

The first convocation of the Delhi University was held in the Assembly Hall here on 26 March 1923 with 750 invitees. Mahatma Gandhi visited Delhi in March 1919 and heard a debate in the historical chamber of the Old Secretariat. Luminaries such as Motilal Nehru, Maulana Abul Kalam and Mohammad Ali Jinnah also debated here.

Archaeological Museum

LOCATION: Inside Guru Gobind Singh Indraprastha University Campus, Kashmere Gate.

SIGNIFICANCE: Originally built in 1637, it underwent renovation after 1803 under the British. Circular pillars form the facade of the building. Two carved sandstone pillars make up part of the entrance gateway.

EXPLICATION: The Museum that has Delhi's early history on display was originally the library of Dara Shikoh, the eldest and favourite son of Shahjahan. This building has the distinction of having been the residence of Ali Mardan Khan (Shahjahan's architect) and later of David Ochterlony, the first British Resident. It housed the Government College from 1804 to 1877.

Dara Shikoh's library

The library originally belonged to Dara Shikoh, the elder brother of Aurangzeb. He was murdered by Aurangzeb in 1659. The British captured the building after defeating the Marathas in 1803 and established a Residency in it. During the Mutiny, the building was looted and all the books in the library, some dating back to Dara Shikoh's time, were destroyed.

Gateway of British Magazine

LOCATION: Lothian Road, Kashmere Gate.

SIGNIFICANCE: Built in the 1820s, the original marble plaque marking the former gate of the magazine can be seen. The British gateway originally led to the magazine, which functioned as an ammunition depot.

EXPLICATION: There are two gateways with semi-octagonal projections on both sides that lead to a vaulted gateway flanked by two small rooms. A marble plaque has inscribed on it the names of the soldiers of the Bengal Artillery who died while defending the magazine in 1857. A domed roof with semi circular arches, *lakhori* bricks and arched niches forms an important feature of the monument.

Mutiny Memorial

LOCATION : Near Bara Hindu Rao Hospital, Civil Lines.

SIGNIFICANCE : Built in1863 on the site of Taylor's Battery during the siege of Delhi in 1857, the memorial honours the soldiers of the Delhi Field Force who were killed during the Mutiny (First War of Independence).

EXPLICATION: The memorial, also known as Fatehgarh or Ajitgarh Memorial, is built in the shape of an octagonal tower of tapering red sandstone rising from a two-tiered platform with an internal staircase. It is located 200 m south from the Ashoka Pillar. On 15 August 1972, the Government of Delhi declared it a protected monument. It is now rededicated to the soldiers who fought the British during the Mutiny. The name of the units, officers, ranks and numbers of British and Indian soldiers killed during the Mutiny are inscribed on slabs around the tower.

Road between Fatehpuri Masjid and Red Fort that marks Chandni Chowk. Formerly a canal used to flow through this area. Now a river of traffic has replaced the canal.

The present occupants of Lala Chunnamal's historic haveli.

CHAPTER 2

Grandeur AND Style

Ages passed
And I did not remember you,
Yet it would be wrong to say
That I had forgotten you.
— Firaq

Shahjahanabad is home to a number of grand and stately havelis of considerable architectural merit constructed along a set pattern. Built during the late Mughal and Colonial periods, the facades are magnificently carved in buff and red sandstone. The fronts of the havelis are decorated with floral patterns, sculptures and fluted designs. The interior of the havelis have a central courtyard around which rooms are built in what is known as the central courtyard plan. One side

usually has a small stone stairway leading to the first floor. The distinguishing features are the grand old wooden doors with iron or brass and copper fittings with intricate designs on them and arched niches.

The wall, the rooms, the arch-vault jack roofs and arcaded verandas are said to represent colonial features. Beautiful *jharokhas* (windows), *chattris* (umbrellas), small decorative balconies, fluted columns, well-designed *chabutras* (platforms), traditional *baithaks* (drawing rooms) and marble floors are features of the Mughal architectural styles. The havelis are set on a high platform above street level. Fine and detailed fluted designs depicting different themes adorn the interiors of these havelis. The use of stained-glass windows, generally associated with churches, is another special feature of these grand residences.

Most havelis have a distinctly marked outer area. The nobleman or owner conducted his routine work and attended to official business here. The inner area constituted the personal living space. The central portion of the building, the *diwankhana*, acted as the drawing room. As imitations of imperial constructions, havelis also had a profusion of gardens, fountains and fruit trees. Today one can hardly visualize such splendour.

It is often overlooked that the Hindu and Muslim mansions had little to differentiate them, even as the owner's perception of life and his beliefs mostly influenced haveli architecture. The havelis were not built at random spots, but in suitable surroundings. The terraces were planned with a sense of purpose: apart from providing privacy. *Khus* (aromatic grass) screens, kept constantly moist, helped keep the summer heat away while the fine stone screens with beautifully worked geometric patterns served as ventilators. Some of the large rooms had fireplaces; the smaller ones were heated with *sigris* (charcoal braziers) full of red-hot coals. Patterned stonework embellished the ceramic tiles, but these are rarely seen now.

A visitor to Shahjahanabad is faced with an entire culture in ruins. The Indian saying that 'not even a bird had the audacity to venture into a haveli' was an apt observation then. Paradoxically, exactly the reverse is true today. The havelis—at least those that remain—have only birds as visitors. Such is the decay that the *tehkhanas* or basements of most of the havelis either stink of sewage or are used as dumping yards.

With burgeoning commercialization, the

havelis are being converted into shops and small residences, and are rapidly becoming places of commerce. As a consequence of the growing population, the congestion in the area is now so great that one can barely walk even on Shahjahanabad's broadest streets. Today, the magnificent havelis of yore are known by a mere house number and their locality. It takes lots of imagination to get an idea of the original boundaries and size of the grand mansions.

What is perhaps most painful is the denial of the architectural and cultural legacy by the owners/inheritors of what was truly a glorious past. There are many who have moved away from Shahjahanabad but visit it daily because their commercial establishments, shops and warehouses are in the Walled City.

The past is disappearing rapidly and without a trace. That, of course, is the common fate of most things belonging to the past. Making way for new functional values that are perceived as being more important is creating a Shahjahanabad that is not averse to demolishing its old culture that was once its very identity. Although, the methods required to restore these buildings are available, implementation of the same is the need of the hour to save Shahjahanabad's distinctiveness and

preserve it for the future. The proverbial 'silver lining'—despite the depredation—is that the past still lives with the present in the most innovative ways in Shahjahanabad.

Thankfully, some of the cultural and traditional values of the place are still visible. People still sit on *gaddis* or thin floor cushions, dress in dhotis and *kurtas* (long shirts) and share a passion for *paan* (betel leaf). The local dialects, the sounds of the *kuchas* and *mohallas* where daily life unfolds at its own pace completely unaware of the outside world, makes the place unique.

> *'Boo-e gul, naalaa-e dil, dood-e chiraagh-e mehfil;*
> *Jo teri bazm se niklaa so pareshaan niklaa.*
> (The flower's scent, the lament of aching hearts, the candle's smoke: He who left your embrace, left distressed.)'
>
> —Ghalib

It is a distress that needs to be visibly assuaged. Only then will a magnificent cultural realm be salvaged. *'Kasra zindgani shad bashad ki dar shab-e-jahan abad bashad.'* (The man who fortunately finds residence in the city of Shahjahanabad leads a happy life). It is innovativeness and a fresh outlook that is important today if one is to move forward and stake a claim to the above verse.

GRAND HAVELIS

1. A *jharokha* from Haveli Khazanchi.
2. Haveli in Kucha Pati Ram.
3. Once an Ayurvedic dispensary at 945, Zorawar Singh Marg, Tilak Gali.
4. Haveli Begum Samroo now houses the Central Bank of India in Bhagirath Place.
5. Haveli Cheera Khana.
6. Doorway to Residence 2664, Churiwalan.

Ramnath Inderdevi Dharamshala

LOCATION: 2764, Chhatta Pratap Singh, Kinari Bazaar, Chandni Chowk.

SIGNIFICANCE: Built in 1850, the Ramnath Inderdevi Dharamshala is a place for public ceremonies and functions. Ramnath was one of the most famous moneylenders of his time. Inderdevi was his wife. The building was meant to be a family residence, but as times changed the functional value of the building also changed.

EXPLICATION: The building has an elaborate, late Mughal facade with a carved sandstone gateway reflecting floral motifs and decorative patterns. The pointed arched entrance has decorative side platforms that lead to an entrance vestibule which, in turn, leads to a courtyard. The courtyard has a three-arched *dalan* (courtyard surrounded by arcaded verandah) with *Shahjahani* fluted columns and pilasters; on the first floor there is a projecting balcony made of buff-coloured sandstone. The initial area of the building was greater than what survives today.

Haveli Haider Quli

LOCATION: 507, Haider Quli, Chandni Chowk.

SIGNIFICANCE: Built in 1916 on the central courtyard plan, the haveli is part of a large mansion of the late Mughal period. Once Haider Quli Khan, Commander of Artillery in the reign of Muhammad Shah, lived a splendid life here. The original mansion was ruined over time.

EXPLICATION: The haveli is entered through an ornamented semi-circular arched gateway. The two-storeyed building has colourful mouldings on the wall that have ceramic tiles with an exquisite rose design. The projecting first-floor balcony shows designs with stone brackets.

A conservation award

The haveli belongs to the Moda family; the name Kedarnath Moda is inscribed on the exterior wall. The family, which is also associated with charitable institutions like the Shri Marwari Aushadhalaya and the Shri Marwari Public Library, has played a significant role in preserving the heritage it owns. The haveli has been awarded the Delhi Development Authority (DDA) Urban Heritage Award for being well maintained.

Features Of Haveli Architecture

1. Brackets
2. Decorative Window
3. Balcony
4. Dyodi
5. Arched Motifs
6. Ganesha Motif
7. Sandstone Pillar
8. Arched Niche
9. Fountain
10. Courtyard
11. Baithak (floor sitting style)
12. Dalan
13. Platform
14. Stained Glass Window
15. Jharokha
16. Swastika
17. Rooftop Terrace
18. Staircase
19. Lakhori Bricks
20. Gali
21. Chajjja

Lala Chunnamal ki Haveli

LOCATION: Main Road, Katra Neel, Chandni Chowk.

SIGNIFICANCE: Built around 1857, Chunnamal's Haveli suffered little damage during the turbulent days of the Mutiny. The grand haveli where shops now occupy the ground floor is largely intact and in its original state. The building has a very large frontage and has been built around two courtyards.

EXPLICATION: The haveli has a high ceiling with decorative and embroidered silk cloth covering the whole area. Large metallic mirrors on two facing walls accentuate the marvellous architecture, while the arched decorative fireplace—still functional after more than a hundred and sixty years—exhibits a multitude of colourful patterns. The decorative chandeliers, the tile work, and the candelabra add to the magnificence of the haveli.

A mosque for Rs 39,000

When the first municipality was formed in 1862, Lala Chunnamal was appointed Municipal Commissioner. In 1864, the British appointed him the Honorary Magistrate of Delhi and he became a founder of the Anglo-Sanskrit School. His haveli even functioned as an extension of the local administrative headquarters. Lala Chunnamal and his family were in the brocade, textiles and money-lending business and supplied these goods to the *toshakhana* (treasury) of the Mughals. Lala Chunnamal bought the Fatehpuri Mosque in 1860 for Rs 39,000. It remained his property until 1877, when Lord Lytton restored it to the Muslims in return for four villages to Lala Chunnamal.

Havelis in Naughara

LOCATION: 2003, Naughara Kinari Bazaar, Chandni Chowk.

SIGNIFICANCE: Built in the early nineteenth century these havelis of immense architectural merit still reflect the superior craftsmanship in sandstone facades and doorways. The havelis still maintain much of their traditional appearance.

EXPLICATION: Built around a central courtyard, these havelis in Naughara (literally, the nine houses) have rooms with high ceilings, arched ornamental gateways and stained glass work. On the first floor, the rooms (with traditional wood and stonework) are still superior pieces of architecture. The sandstone brackets, an arched entrance with floral carvings and the design as a whole are indeed commendable. The nine houses and the temple located within this enclosure have a unity in appearance and style with courtyards, ornamental gateways and a wooden balcony with stone brackets.

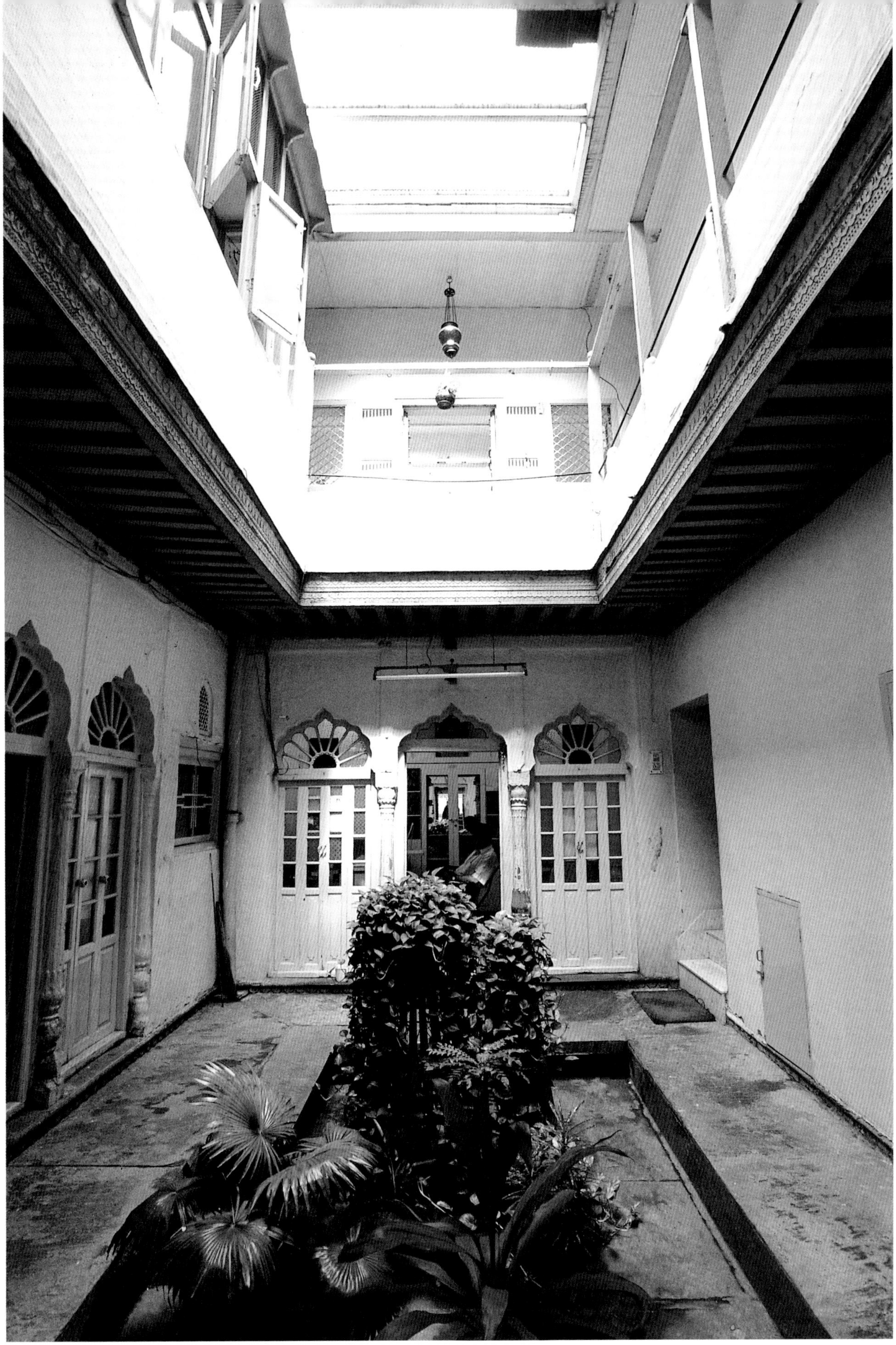

Haveli Katra Khushal Rai

LOCATION: 1961, Katra Khushal Rai, Kinari Bazaar.

SIGNIFICANCE: This haveli has an arched, elaborately carved buff-coloured sandstone gateway representing superior craftsmanship.

EXPLICATION: The facade of the haveli—said to be built in 1850—is decorated with floral patterns and designs around arched niches. The house is built around a central courtyard with arched doors on all sides painted in different colours. There is a projecting balcony on the first floor, which has medallions on the parapet depicting the sun and the moon as auspicious symbols. The haveli, used for residential and commercial purposes, has had a few modifications made to it, especially an extra floor, though it continues to retain a traditional aura.

Secluded spaces

Chajjas (balconies) and decorative or wooden grills on the first floor form an integral part of haveli architecture. In days gone by, these features enabled family members, especially ladies, to view fairs, festivals and city processions. The narrow streets also made communication between neighbours easy and frequent.

Haveli Vakilpura

LOCATION: 1307, Vakilpura, Gali Guliyan, Chandni Chowk.

SIGNIFICANCE: Built in 1924, this residential-cum-commercial building is an elaborately carved buff-coloured sandstone structure, representing a plethora of designs on the walls and arched doorways.

EXPLICATION: This double-storeyed building has an arched sandstone facade with curious carvings on the pillars and decorative features on the entrance. Another distinctive feature is the height of the ceilings, which ranges upto fifteen feet. Built on the central courtyard plan, the rooms with large semicircular arched windows are now used for commercial purposes.

Haveli Churiwalan

LOCATION: 2549, Churiwalan, Chandni Chowk (now a free Homeopathic dispensary).

SIGNIFICANCE: Built in 1903 by Lala Ram Saran 'Tasveer Wale', this haveli was awarded the Delhi Development Authority (DDA) Urban Heritage Award for its unique character regarding art and architecture.

EXPLICATION: Built on the central courtyard plan , the haveli has a carved arched sandstone facade with doorways that are at least a hundred years old. Around the courtyard are rooms with old stained glass work and designed ceramic tiles arranged in a symmetrical fashion. Sandstone brackets with intricate carvings lend magnificence to the projecting first-floor balcony. With time, even as the style of living has changed, the original character of the building has been well preserved. The circular pillars, the arched platform and the quaint, old windows contribute to its splendour. The front portion of the house now serves as a free dispensary.

Dharamshala Rai Sahib
Lala Laxmi Narayan

LOCATION: 2/8, Church Mission Road, Fatehpuri, Chandni
Chowk.

SIGNIFICANCE: Built in 1906 this building reflects a
traditional architectural style.

EXPLICATION: Constructed according to the central courtyard
plan, it has an elaborately carved, pointed and arched
sandstone gateway and sixty-six big rooms with good
craftsmanship in wood and stone work.

For weary travellers

Chandni Chowk or the Walled City has the largest number of dharmashalas in Delhi. These are used for
social and community-related functions. Mostly built by the *Vaishya* community (the business class),
these dharmashalas provide boarding and lodging for a nominal charge or for free.

Haveli Ram Kutiya

LOCATION: 504, Kucha Pati Ram, Sita Ram Bazaar, Chandni Chowk.

SIGNIFICANCE: Built in 1915 by Lala Kanhiya Lal and known as Ram Kutiya this double-storeyed mansion has a stately buff-coloured sandstone facade with a reflecting arched entrance and decorative windows that project outwards on the ground floor.

EXPLICATION: The haveli has a large courtyard with an old working fountain. The rooms on the left have a veranda with rectangular sandstone columns. The beautiful *jharoka* on the arched entrance is made of wood and sandstone. The rooms of the haveli still exude the aura of a bygone era with a beautifully designed fireplace, arched niches and impressive wooden doorways.

Kokan Mal Ki Haveli

LOCATION: 550, Kucha Pati Ram, Sita Ram Bazaar, Chandni Chowk.
SIGNIFICANCE: Built in 1890 by the father of Shri Kokan Mal Johari, a socially active person, who was the trustee of the Ramlila Committee and of about eighty other institutions. He was in the diamond trade, though during the Mutiny, he lost most of his property and business.
EXPLICATION: The haveli is situated on a high platform and has a semi-circular arched sandstone gateway. It has a central courtyard with semi-circular arched rooms on all the sides in the original style of the havelis. The large sandstone frontage is a brilliant piece of architecture. There is an extensive use of sandstone in the construction of this haveli, although, the walls are made up of bricks, with a narrow staircase leading to the upper floors.

Haveli Kucha Pati Ram

LOCATION: 962, Kucha Pati Ram, Sita Ram Bazaar, Chandni Chowk.

SIGNIFICANCE: Built during the early twentieth century, this two-storeyed building is constructed in the traditional haveli style with semi-circular arched openings. A notable feature is the brilliant craftsmanship on buff-coloured sandstone.

EXPLICATION: The ground floor on both sides of the haveli has a highly ornamental facade. Human figures adorn the door panels, floral patterns in buff-coloured sandstone and a projecting balcony supported by well-finished sandstone brackets are considered architectural gems. The parapet on the terrace is colonial in fashion. The owners have been living in this house since its construction, though their lifestyle and the functional value of the haveli has changed.

Pyarelal Madhoram Dharamshala

LOCATION: 1042, Main Road, Sita Ram Bazaar, Chandni Chowk.

SIGNIFICANCE: Built in 1921, the dharmashala has sandstone figures carved on the arched entrance, while floral patterns and elephant motifs along with symbolic images of the sun and the moon add to its beauty.

EXPLICATION: The frontal sandstone entrance has sculpted figurines, such as Lord Ganesha in the middle flanked by the sun and the moon along with floral decorations. On either side of the carved gateway is a small room with an opening at the level of the ventilator. The gateway opens into an entrance vestibule leading to an open courtyard with *dalans* and four arched openings. The interior of the place is designed with a fine aesthetic sense. The first-floor level is used for residential purposes. The portraits of Lala Pyarelal Madhoram and subsequent trustees adorn the wall of the ground floor.

Haksar ki Haveli

LOCATION: Prem Narain Road, Bazaar Sita Ram, Chandni Chowk.
SIGNIFICANCE: The Haksar haveli was where India's first Prime
Minister Pandit Jawaharlal Nehru married Kamla Kaul, in February
1916. The Haksars—then the most distinguished Kashmiri family
in Delhi—had lent this haveli for the marriage to Kamla Nehru's
parents.
EXPLICATION: The haveli, now in ruins, has a cusped, arched
sandstone entrance gateway with two *jharokhas* on either side and
an inscription. Fish motifs, considered auspicious, are part of the
decorative features. Inside there are fluted sandstone columns
and a portion of the *lakhori* brick wall.

Haveli Ballimaran

LOCATION: 3014, near Choti Baradari, Ballimaran, Chandni Chowk.

SIGNIFICANCE: Dating back to the later Mughal period, this grand haveli is said to have belonged to the erstwhile Nawab of Jhajjar. It has a central courtyard plan with exquisite craftsmanship on the sandstone columns and the facade.

EXPLICATION: The haveli has a now-dilapidated arched sandstone facade. The vestibule leads to an impressive courtyard with a peepal tree in the premises. The upper floor of the haveli is decorated with beautifully carved buff-coloured sandstone *jharokhas* (windows) on both sides of the *baradari* (a colonnaded building usually with twelve openings, see below). The main portion has floral patterns and designs on the facade and beautiful carvings on the *jaalis* and brackets. The pillars have elaborately designed bases. The basement of the haveli, however, is in a poor condition. Until a few years ago, this haveli was used for family welfare activities under the name of the Madan Mohan Malviya Mahila Shilp Vidyalaya.

Pandit Bihari Lal ki Haveli

LOCATION: 505, Kucha Pati Ram, Sita Ram Bazaar, Chandni Chowk.

SIGNIFICANCE: Built in 1926-1927 by Pandit Bihari Lal, an executive engineer from the Benaras Hindu University. The haveli is double storeyed with extensive stone carving on the arched sandstone facade.

EXPLICATION: The haveli, built around a central courtyard on 350 square yards, has two large decorative windows on either side of the entrance. The balcony on the first floor has a wood finish and has a marble floor. The interior of the haveli has stained glass windows over the doorways. The auspicious symbol in Hinduism, 'Om', is etched on the front arched entrance. This area has a number of havelis of architectural merit. The similarity of their architectural style is an indicator of the living harmony between the inhabitants.

Haveli Dharampura

LOCATION: 2293, Dharampura, Chandni Chowk.

SIGNIFICANCE: Built in the late nineteenth century, the haveli along with several of its contemporaries, has an original sandstone facade.

EXPLICATION: Built around the central courtyard plan, it still has arched decorative patterns, floral carvings and designs in the interior portion. The building has a high plinth with a decorative facade, while the exquisite floral carvings and the elaborate wooden door add to the beauty of the building. The rooms have cusped, arched circular pillars. A projecting balcony on the first floor is still in use. Lime mortar has been added along with the *lakhori* bricks to lend strength to the haveli.

Haveli Kucha Ghasi Ram

LOCATION: 316, Kucha Ghasi Ram, Chandni Chowk.

SIGNIFICANCE: This is a late Mughal period haveli, which forms part of the many houses of Bhawani Shankar. Munshi Bhawani Shankar was a *khattri* who acquired power and wealth during the Maratha occupation of Delhi. He was notoriously disloyal to the Marathas on account of his shady dealings with the British.

EXPLICATION: This large and imposing house has a stunning, ornamental gateway as well as an arched sandstone facade with beautiful decorative features. These include a designed platform, arched niches and stone brackets. The large rooms are built around a central courtyard which once had a magnificent fountain. The haveli still has its original iron-studded gateway.

Namak Haram ki Haveli

The British gave Munshi Bhawani Shankar a pension which was enjoyed by his descendants. His house began to be called Namak Haram ki Haveli (literally, the mansion of one not true to his salt, and hence a traitor). The Munshi was incensed and complained to his English masters, whereupon a general proclamation was issued that forbade people from calling the family Namak Haram.

Haveli Krishna Gali

LOCATION: 115, Krishna Gali, Paharganj.

SIGNIFICANCE: Built in the nineteenth century, this haveli is another architectural jewel.

EXPLICATION: This double-storeyed building has a projecting balcony on the upper floor with overhead circular projections. Built around a central courtyard, the walls of the interior have religious and mythological paintings. The arched niches and pierced screen work on the sandstone blocks are some other significant features. The sculpted figure of a man stands guard on the front entrance. Ornamental windows and semi-circular, arched sandstone decorative patterns on the wall add to the beauty of the building. This is the only haveli of its kind in the entire area.

Lala Ambey Prasad ki Haveli

LOCATION: 1200, Kucha Pati Ram, Chandni Chowk.

SIGNIFICANCE: Built in 1927 by Lala Ambey Prasad , this haveli has a truly stately presence.

EXPLICATION: Built around a central courtyard plan, the haveli originally had a drawing room decorated with glass work and a balcony on the first floor. It also has beautiful carvings, and Hindu-style architecture is strongly reflected in the structure. It has a sandstone facade with floral motifs and designs. Exquisite carvings on the front depict Lord Krishna, Lord Rama and Lord Hanuman and the five Pandava brothers of the *Mahabharata*. Several carvings highlight the importance given to women during that time. Lala Ambey Prasad was also a trustee at Garh Mukteshwara, a famous Hindu shrine. It is said that the sets for the famous film, *Mughal-e-Azam*, were inspired by this haveli.

Residence Nicholson Road

LOCATION: 3490, Nicholson Road, Kashmere Gate.

SIGNIFICANCE: Built in 1935 with bricks and lime mortar, originally the residence of a Muslim family, the mansion was purchased by Shri Fakir Chand Sabbarwal in 1959. Fakir Chand was a prominent businessman in Rawalpindi who migrated to Delhi during the Partition. This double-storeyed building built in the early twentieth century has a stately carved front reflecting both colonial and other typical haveli features.

EXPLICATION: Famous as Asha Mansion, the building boasts of oriental designs, pillars, arches, large sandstone carvings and beautiful ceramic tiles. According to the traditional style, the name of the owners and the year of construction are inscribed on the front. The rooms have high ceilings and floral patterns. Built opposite the city wall, the building provides a striking contrast between the past and the present.

Haveli Shamnath Marg

LOCATION: 17, Shamnath Marg, Civil Lines, Delhi.

SIGNIFICANCE: Built in 1902 by Lala Shriram, the son of Rai Bahadur Madan Gopal, a well-known Barrister. The family traces its roots to Raja Todarmal (he was one of the nine jewels of Akbar's court, who was a legendary land reformer).

EXPLICATION: The architecture of this mansion reflects a strong colonial influence. It has circular pillars, mouldings, an arched entrance, high ceilings and a well-maintained courtyard with a fountain and a well. The house has three bedrooms and a drawing room. Antiques such as metal sculptures, period furniture and beautiful glass artefacts can be found. The family still has the original documents of the mansion pertaining to the British period, with the signatures of Lord Metcalfe.

Lala Sanwal Dass Ram Roop Dharamshala

LOCATION: Gali Ram Roop, Subzi Mandi

SIGNIFICANCE: Built in 1939 by Lala Sanwal Dass Ram Roop the dharmashala has an elaborately carved triple-storeyed gateway opening on to the main street.

EXPLICATION: The sandstone entrance has sculpted mythological figures along with exquisitely carved sandstone *jharokhas* flanking a large central arch which encloses the semi-circular entrance. The interior of the dharmashala has rooms along a central courtyard. Floral patterns, sun motifs with symbolic images of peacocks add to the building.

Haveli Zeenat Mahal

LOCATION: Zeenat Mahal, Lal Kuan.

SIGNIFICANCE : Built by the last Mughal, Emperor Bahadur Shah Zafar for his favourite wife, Zeenat Mahal, this haveli was once imposing and beautiful. In the year 1886 the empress died in Rangoon where she was living on a measly pension of five hundred rupees.

EXPLICATION: The haveli was built as a residence for the paternal family of the empress. Beautiful projecting *jharokhas*, an ornamental ceiling and medallions in the spandrels of the arch are some remanents of its glorious past. An imposing gateway is all that remains intact of the haveli today.

Beautiful decorations in the Shwetambar-Naughara Jain Temple.

CHAPTER 3

Houses OF Worship

C handni Chowk is an abiding symbol of universal brotherhood and religious harmony. Since the time of its inception it has welcomed different faiths and traditions. The same, in fact, is true of the whole of Shahjahanabad.

The Chowk occupies a unique position in the world. Within its vicinity are found temples, mosques, churches and gurdwaras—testifying to the seamless co-existence of all faiths. This co-existence is not limited to faith alone but extends into all spheres of life.

To avoid being sucked into its present chaos visitors often avoid entering the city. However, to absorb its liveliness it is necessary to walk in its streets . Its countless lanes and bylanes hide within their folds several serene spots that lend moments of peace in the midst of a

fast-paced modern world. Viewed thus the city illuminates the concept of 'Unity in Diversity' most brilliantly.

During the Mughal period, festivals in Shahjahanabad centred round the tombs of Sufi saints and mystics. Fairs and festivals like Dussehra and *Ramleela* were other occasions for religious celebrations. During the sixteenth century, devotional practices at the shrines of Sufi saints were similar to those of Hindu practices. Gifts (not strictly material) were offered, candles lit, devotional songs sung and matters of the spirit discussed among the devotees. These shrines were centres of sanctity and bestowed the 'peace that passeth all understanding'. It was assumed that at these shrines, pilgrims of any religious persuasion received the spiritual benevolence of the saint—who was seen as an active communicator between God and those who petitioned Him. All those who were distraught would find his grace.

Shahjahanabad's religious monuments, however, were not just an integral part of various religions. They represented, as they still do, architectural and art styles and the social and economic features of the period during which they were built.

Today, Shahjahanabad easily fuses the religious with the secular. Places of culture, art and religion have become the mainstay of people's livelihood. It is from their vicinity that the residents of Old Delhi carry on their major occupation: trading. The mosques, for instance, are on the first floor while the shops occupy the ground floor. The revenue earned from the shops is used for the maintenance of the mosques. Mosques have always been in preponderance in the *katras* and *kuchas* of Shahjahanabad. Red sandstone has been extensively used in building the monuments. Some of their domes were gilded with copper. The Sunehri Masjid has, in fact, a golden dome (*sunehri* literally means golden). Most mosques have inscriptions from the Quran. In many cases the inscription on the mosque points to the concept behind its construction. Through these inscriptions, the builder highlighted the ideas of the king and the faith that the monarch and his noblemen professed. Sometimes, of course, the inscriber added a word or so about himself. Some inscriptions start with the titles Champion of the Faith, Cherisher of the People or Doer of Justice. Some inscriptions went a step further and had references like The Rising Place of the Sun or mentioned Alexander the

Great. The explanations behind these inscriptions are now lost and so they remain interesting oddities. Imposing gateways along with courtyards and domes are distinguishing features of the mosques.

The other major structures are temples with beautiful, delicately carved doorways surmounted by a domed balcony or sporting a porch. Inside carved doorways, staircases lead to an elevated marble courtyard surrounded by a colonnade with marble pillars. The ceilings are adorned with paintings that are hundreds of years old, detailing religious symbols, such as the peacock. Floral carvings are strewn on the colonnades, every inch of them painted delicately and elaborately. Most temples lie in narrow lanes and bylanes which are filled with devotees. Adjacent to the temple an old mansion or a workshop lends an old-world charm to the quaintness of the busy lanes.

The temples of the two sects of the Jains—the Digambars (sky-clad or naked) as well as the Shwetambars (white-clad), have marvellous art and architecture. Under the high dome one finds a beautiful altar for the idol, which sits serenely ten to thirty feet under it.

Churches also occupy an important place among the houses of worship in Shahjahanabad. They stand as silent testimonials to a bygone era and form an integral part of the religious realm of Shahjahanabad. Most were built during the early period of British occupation. Prominent among them, and one of the largest, is St. James Church. If stones could speak, this church would have several stories to tell. The 1857 sepoys, for instance, shot at the bell and cross of the church hoping that if they fell, ruin would befall the English.

The other religious structures belong to Sikhism, a religion that is an integral part of Chandni Chowk. Guru Teg Bahadur, the ninth Sikh guru, was martyred here, under a banyan tree in 1675. Today, *Guru ka Langar* (the community kitchen), which provides free meals to all, and the *Prakash Utsav* (Light Festival) are among some of the important cultural traditions celebrated (in the Chowk) at Gurudwara Sis Ganj.

The Walled City is a sacred space in itself, yet its religious heritage, under pressure from consumerism, is eroding rather rapidly. The city could easily have been one of those places in modern Delhi where one could explore the meaning of life since it lies some distance away from the march towards materialism. It still is one place where life cannot be severed from faith.

St. Mary's Church

LOCATION: S.P. Mukherjee Marg, Presentation Convent School Complex, Chandni Chowk.

SIGNIFICANCE: Built in 1865, the church was laid out in a cruciform plan with the arms of the building in a semi-circular shape.

EXPLICATION: At the entrance of the church one finds a semi-circular arched decorative gateway and a bell tower. The blind arcade on the first floor is a special feature of the church. The interior of the church has some magnificent decorative features such as stained glass windows and mouldings. The Ten Commandments written inside the church are an added attraction.

Mosque and Dargah Shah Ghulam Ali

LOCATION: 2358, Kucha Mir Hashim, Turkman Gate.

SIGNIFICANCE: The mosque dates back to 1781 and the *dargah* (tomb) to 1824. Shah Ghulam Ali was a disciple of Saint Mirza Mazhar-i-Janjanan. Shah Ghulam Ali was buried here in 1824.

EXPLICATION: The two-bay deep mosque has three bulbous domes with black marble strips and a cusped arched entrance. There are small minarets on all the four corners. The *dargah* has beautiful lattice screens. The enclosure has a total of four graves with a large dome over it. The central grave on the platform is that of Shah Ghulam Ali. The inscription at the head of the grave of Maulvi Rahim Baksh is a quotation from the Quran.

Hanuman Mandir

LOCATION: 1737, Chowk Shah Mubarak, Ajmeri Gate.
SIGNIFICANCE: Built by the ancestors of Shri Gulab Chand Rohtagi.
EXPLICATION: The temple has a semi-circular arched entrance made of sandstone, where one finds a representation of the cosmic features in the figures of the sun and the moon. Its facade is made of stone with beautiful carvings and mythological representations from different faiths. It has a scene from the Hindu epic, *Mahabharata*, and also one depicting the first Sikh Guru, Sri Guru Nanak Dev. The floral carvings along with the sculpted figurines on the facade add to the temple's divine charm.

Dedicated to courage

The temple is dedicated to Guru Sant Charan Dass, who is said to have confronted Nadir Shah when he came to plunder Delhi.

Ghaziuddin ki Masjid

LOCATION: Anglo-Arabic Public School, Ajmeri Gate.

SIGNIFICANCE: Built in 1727 this elegant mosque is a replica of the Jami Mosque of Lahore, but built on a smaller scale. It is named after Ghaziuddin Khan, an extremely successful and highly respected military commander in Aurangzeb's army, whose son eventually became the first Nizam of Hyderabad.

EXPLICATION: The mosque has seven arches with the central archway dominating the facade. The red sandstone building has white marble relief work and three domes with impressive octagonal *chattris* and minarets.

Masjid Hauz Qazi

LOCATION: Hauz Qazi Chowk, Chandni Chowk.

SIGNIFICANCE: Originally the Bagh-i-Nabiullah, Hazrat Khwaza Mohammad Nabiullah built a garden and a mosque in 1718-19.

EXPLICATION: The mosque has a decorative arched gateway, the ceiling is painted in many colours. As the name signifies, this mosque houses an 'auspicious' fountain in its courtyard that has a stone inscription on its rear wall. Atop the arched *dalan* there is an inscription in white marble. The five-bay mosque is two-bay deep with the arches supported by circular columns. The fountain is made up of sandstone and is adorned with decorative features in silver and organic colours. It is said that in areas adjacent to where the mosque stands, there was once a garden. The present mosque was reconstructed at the same time as the garden was laid out and the inscription on its entrance put up.

Amrud Wali Masjid

LOCATION: Near Rehmani Building, Bulbulikhana, Bazaar Sita Ram, Chandni Chowk.

SIGNIFICANCE: This three-storeyed mosque, built in 1735-36, is also known as Masjid Maulvi Qutubuddin, after the person who repaired it.

EXPLICATION: The mosque has shops on the ground floor. It has five beautiful cusped arched entrances made of sandstone that have floral carvings and exquisite designs on them. The sandstone pillars with decorative features are indeed marvellous. There is an inscription in the mosque stating: 'The Masjid has been built with due elegance. Shah Hussain has built a mosque and school.'

Artist's rendition of Sunehri Masjid (Golden Mosque: c. 1721)

Seat of Nadir Shah

Nadir Shah was one of the most notorious plunderers of Delhi. It was here that Nadir Shah took his seat after ordering a general massacre of the inhabitants of Delhi on 22 March 1739. This was also the spot where he was solicited to desist from the massacre.

Sunehri Masjid

LOCATION: Opposite Bhai Mati Das Chowk, near the Fountain, Chandni Chowk.

SIGNIFICANCE: Raushan-ud-Daula Zafar Khan built this mosque in 1721-22. The Sunehri Masjid literally the golden mosque has domes covered in gilded copper. These shine like gold, hence the popular name.

EXPLICATION: The mosque stands on a masonry platform with shops on the ground floor. There are three arched entrances to the mosque leading into three rooms covered by domes sheathed with gilded copper and finials.

St. James Church

LOCATION: Kashmere Gate, South of Inter State Bus Terminus.

SIGNIFICANCE: The first church commissioned by the British is based on the Greek Cross plan. Built in 1836 by James Skinner, it is a fine example of classic, colonial architecture.

EXPLICATION: The church, based on the Greek Cross plan, consists of a central octagonal space covered with a Florentine dome mounted by a lantern. The decorative features include stained glass showing Jesus Christ. The mouldings and parapets along with the organ add to the church's splendour.

A vow fulfilled

Born in 1778, James Skinner was the son of a Scottish soldier and a Rajput mother. He vowed to build a church when he was seriously injured and was lying on his deathbed during one of the battles. Stanley Skinner, a descendant of James Skinner, donated four bells to the Church.

Fakhr-ul-Mosque

LOCATION: 1270-75, Bara Bazaar, Kashmere Gate.

SIGNIFICANCE: Built in 1728–29 by Kaniz-i-Fatima (titled Fakr-i-Jahan) in memory of her husband Shujaat Khan.

EXPLICATION: The mosque stands on a 2.5-metre high platform, which has a number of shops on it. The marble dome has alternate black and white strips. The mosque is flanked by minarets and surmounted by octagonal open cupolas with gilded domes and pinnacles. It has three rooms, each of which are entered through arched entrances surmounted by domes.

Commander Khan

Shujaat Khan was a noble in the court of Aurangzeb. He began his career as commander of Akbarabad (Agra) Fort and rose to the post of commander of the artillery. His real name was Rag Andaz Beg, Shiyaat Khan being the title given to him in 1672-73.

Ghata Masjid or Zinat-ul-Masjid

LOCATION: Kharati Ghat, Ring Road, Daryaganj.

SIGNIFICANCE: Zinat-ul-Nisa Begum, the daughter of Aurangzeb, built the masjid in 1707. She is buried inside the tomb in the complex. The tomb was removed after 1857 when the British used the mosque for military purposes.

EXPLICATION: The mosque is situated in a commanding position and consists of a prayer chamber with seven arches and three bulbous domes with black strips. There are two large minarets, a courtyard and a central tank facing the riverside. Predominantly made of red sandstone, the mosque is considered a fine example of Islamic architecture. For many years after the Mutiny, the mosque was used as a bakery for British troops.

Gauri-Shankar Temple

LOCATION: Main Road, Chandni Chowk, opposite Red Fort.

SIGNIFICANCE: Appa Gangadhara, a Maratha Brahmin in the service of the Scindias, built the original temple in the late Mughal period, probably in 1761.

EXPLICATION: The temple is devoted to Gauri-Shankar (Gauri is the name of Parvati and Shankar is Lord Shiva; Shiva is also called *Ardhanareeshwara*: half-man and half-woman). There are two images, one of Gauri, the other of Shiva. It is said that the *linga*, a universal symbol of Lord Shiva, inside the temple is eight hundred years old while the facade of the building is new. The ornate work and gilt paintings inside the temple lend a sense of deep serenity. The temple is of considerable importance as in the past it was on the road from the city to the Yamuna bathing ghats. It is still visited by a large number of worshippers throughout the year.

Fatehpuri Masjid

LOCATION: Western end of Chandni Chowk, Shahjahanabad.

SIGNIFICANCE: Built in 1650 the mosque is named after Fatehpuri Begum, one of the wives of Emperor Shahjahan.

EXPLICATION: This red sandstone mosque has a single dome and four corner minarets. The lofty main arch is in the centre of the mosque, flanked by three wings and three scalloped arches on either side. The courtyard is paved with stone slabs and has a large central pool. The complex also has single and double-storeyed apartments used for commercial and residential purposes.

Mosque for debates

Lala Chunnamal, a Hindu, was once the owner of the mosque. He had purchased the mosque for Rs 39,000. Later, on the insistence of the British, he restored it to the Muslims. After the Mutiny, the British closed the mosque. Three years later, in 1860, Muslims were again allowed to use it. The clock on the front of the masjid faces the main road. The Fatehpuri Masjid was the venue of several public debates between Muslim theologians and Christian missionaries in the nineteenth century.(also see pg. 73)

Gurudwara Sis Ganj

LOCATION: Main Road, Chandni Chowk.

SIGNIFICANCE: The gurdwara was built in the memory of Guru Teg Bahadur who was beheaded here in 1675.

EXPLICATION: The three-storeyed gurdwara has a *chattri* on each terrace corner and a large *chattri* in the centre of the facade. The *jaalis*, *jharokhas* and the marble floor inside add to its beauty. A banyan tree marks the spot where the Guru was beheaded. Bhai Mati Dass Museum opposite the gurdwara houses paintings related to Sikhism and is open from 7 a.m. to 7 p.m.; entry is free.

The Guru's martyrdom

Guru Teg Bahadur was in Aurangzeb's prison for forty days. During his inprisonment, he used to sing hymns from the *Adi Grantha*, the holy book of the Sikhs. Guru Teg Bahadur was the son of Guru Hargobind Singh, and the ninth Guru of the Sikhs.

The Mosque in Paharganj

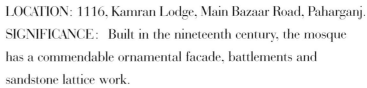

LOCATION: 1116, Kamran Lodge, Main Bazaar Road, Paharganj.

SIGNIFICANCE: Built in the nineteenth century, the mosque has a commendable ornamental facade, battlements and sandstone lattice work.

EXPLICATION: The high domes of the mosque give a unique and picturesque view of the street. The entrance of the building is through an ornamental cusped arch with a projecting *jharokha* ornamented with a canopy. At the terrace level located on the first floor, there is a large central, arched entrance with intricate designs in sandstone.

Digambar Jain Mandir

LOCATION: 1513, Kucha Seth Dariba Kalan, Chandni Chowk.

SIGNIFICANCE: The temple, also known as the Shri Digambar Jain Bada Temple was built in 1834. The double-storeyed temple was constructed by the Jains of Delhi and has some exquisite carvings in the interiors.

EXPLICATION: The temple has a lavishly carved floral-design gateway. In the sanctum sanctorum, on the raised platform of a column is the image of Lord Adinath. There are arched colonnaded halls on three sides. The pillars of the shrine and those in the halls are made of marble; mosaic work is found on the arched niches. The interior of the temple and the ceilings are decorated with miniature paintings representing dancers and divine figurines.

Digambar Jain Lal Mandir

LOCATION: Netaji Subash Marg, opposite Red Fort, Chandni Chowk.

SIGNIFICANCE: The temple, also known as Lashkar-a-Mandir, was built by a Jain in the army of Aurangzeb. According to legend, when Aurangzeb visited the temple, the *nagaras* (drums) started beating on their own—nobody could be seen beating them. Aurangzeb had ordered a ban on the beating of drums in the temple, as the timing of the *Namaz* (Islamic prayers) and the *Abhishek* (devotional prayers) were the same. It is said to be the oldest Jain temple in Shahjahanabad. The original temple was built in 1526 and was further enlarged in the 1870s.

EXPLICATION: The temple has idols of Lord Parshavanath, Lord Adinath and Lord Chandraprabhu in its sanctum sanctorum. It has painted ceilings, designed pillars and an impressive *shikhar* (spire). It has semi-circular arched entrances made of marble. Fluted *Shahjahani* columns and golden-coloured paintings in the complex add serenity to its ambience.

Faith inspires a hospital

The Jains are noted for their non-violence towards any living creature. *Ahimsa* **(non-violence)** is the foundation of their faith. A visible manifestation of their concern is the Charity Bird Hospital—a place where wounded, injured and sick birds are treated.

Shwetambar-
Naughara Jain Temple

LOCATION: 1997, Naughara, Kinari Bazaar, Chandni Chowk.

SIGNIFICANCE: Built in the late Mughal period, and indeed comparable with the
beauty of the Taj Mahal in terms of stucco work and design, this temple, which is also
known as the *jauharis'* (jewellers') temple, is said to have been founded during the time
of Emperor Shahjahan by the Jains.

EXPLICATION: This Jain temple made of white marble has two storeys. The interior of
the temple has decorative arched entrances and gilded paintings representing various
mythological and religious scenes. It also has religious paintings done in gold, green
and yellow. On the doors of the sanctum sanctorum, twenty-four Jain *tirthankaras*
(teachers) are depicted. The exquisite craftsmanship in gold, representing floral
decorations, can hardly be seen elsewhere. The temple interior has fine intricate carvings
on the pillars, and *jaalis* on the arched entrance gateway and on the platform. The
ground floor of the temple functions as a museum. The paintings, most of which were
done during the late Mughal Era, are in gold and use bright, organic colours.

Shri Digambar Jain Naya Mandir

LOCATION: Opposite 2318, Dharampura, Chandni Chowk.

SIGNIFICANCE: Lala Harsukhrai, a councillor of the Raja of Bharatpur, built the Jain temple in 1807. It took seven years to complete.

EXPLICATION: The entrance to the two-storeyed temple is through a sandstone-arched gateway. The centre of the raised platform is crowned by an image of Lord Adinath. The temple is embellished with many mythological and religious images, and a bulbous dome surmounts the main shrine. There are three marble-pillared halls and the shrine and porch have floral decorations. The temple has marvellous sandstone craftsmanship on its gateway, marble pillars and wall paintings. The wall paintings represent scenes that are in keeping with the spirit of Jainism.

Artist's rendition of Jama Masjid (Southern gateway: c. 1650)

Jama Masjid

LOCATION: Near Red Fort, Shahjahanabad.

SIGNIFICANCE: The Jama Masjid, also known as Masjid-i-Jahan Numa and Jumma Masjid, (the word *Jumma* means collective or congregational mosque, and it also stands for Friday), was built by Emperor Shahjahan and is one of the largest mosques in India. Its foundation was laid on 6 October 1650. It is said to be 1000 yards away from the Red Fort.

EXPLICATION: The cost of building the mosque was one million rupees excluding the valuable marble and sandstone. Five thousand workers were employed in its construction and worked continuously for six years. The mosque stands on rocky ground, commonly known as Bhojla Pahari. The courtyard of the mosque is approached from three sides by broad flights of steps made of red sandstone. Three domes ornamented with alternate black and white strips of marble and gilded pinnacles surmount the mosque. Two lofty minarets flank the mosque. The courtyard is paved with red sandstone and has a marble tank in the centre.

All in a day's work

It is said that a mosque is a place of God that is why the level of this mosque is higher than the emperor's throne at Red Fort. An interesting story recounts how the day after the mosque had reached completion on Ramzan Id, Emperor Shahjahan unexpectedly came to say his prayers. However, a lot of rubble was still lying around which would have taken the officials at least a month to clear up. However, the emperor's wish was their command. After much deliberation the authorities decided to issue an invitation to the masses to collect the surplus material. This proclamation met with such unqualified success that the job was completed within a few hours. In the year 1829, Mirza Salim, son of Akbar II, erected a sandstone pulpit under the central entrance of the mosque. It was meant to be a seat for the *mukabbir*, the person who assists the *Imam* (head priest) by giving the duration of time by which the various motions during prayer are regulated.

St. Stephen's Church

LOCATION: Church Mission Road, Fatehpuri, Shahjahanabad.

SIGNIFICANCE: Built in 1867 the church, under the aegis of the Church of North India, was awarded the DDA Urban Heritage Award in 1994.

EXPLICATION: The church has a high bell tower with the central zone separated from the sides by impressive semi-circular arches. The sides have a flat roof. It also has a beautiful old stained glass rose window and Corinthian capitols with superb craftsmanship.

Artist's rendition of Kalan Masjid (c. 1387)

Kaali Masjid or Kalan Masjid

LOCATION: Near Turkman Gate, Shahjahanabad.

SIGNIFICANCE: The mosque was built in 1387 on moderately high ground and, with the exception of the Jama Masjid, is the most prominent structure in Shahjahanabad. Firoz Shah Tughlaq's Principal Minister, Khan-i-Jahan-Junan Shah, built a total of seven mosques, one of which was the Kaali Masjid. Kalan means large in Arabic. Firoz Shah Tughlaq himself ruled for more than twenty-seven years and was one of the most enlightened rulers that India has seen. He is known for improving irrigation in India via a system of canals.

EXPLICATION: The mosque consists of two storeys. Built of common quartzite sandstone, the mosque has thirty steps to the entrance that opens into a square courtyard surrounded by a cloister. The mosque has a prayer chamber, consisting of fine arches supporting fifteen domes in all.

CHAPTER 4

Birds feeding outside the Town Hall.

World OF Work

Man lives in contentment in an environment that suits him best. Thus, institutions and establishments become an inseparable part of any place where man lives and works. Unfortunately, modernization brings in its wake urban development. Shahjahanabad is no different. But since it has a long history, it represents an interesting synthesis of all the ideas that produced architectural wonders in different forms down the ages. The city of Shahjahanabad was not limited just to the area

Habash Khan Ka Phatak

In Mughal days, words like *ghulam* and *qul*, meaning slave, had acquired an everlasting significance. Akbar had issued orders that a slave should be called *chela* (disciple) not *ghulam* or *qul*. In fact Chelon Ka Kucha is synonymous for Houses of Slaves in which, at one time, there were as many as forty houses of the *amirs* or noblemen.

One famous slave was Habash Khan. His real name was Sidi Miftah and he had reached the top of the imperial hierarchy. Habash Khan was a trusted servant of the Nizam Shahi Dynasty, and Shahjahan was impressed with him. At the age of 110, Khan could eat a whole stuffed sheep. He was described as trusted, loyal, bold, strong and pious. He became governor of the strong fort of Udgir in Shahjahan's time. Habash Khan Ka Phatak, and the *kucha* inside the gate, have developed into a very busy shopping centre known today as Tilak Bazaar which is near Khari Baoli. General goods, dyes and chemicals are sold here.

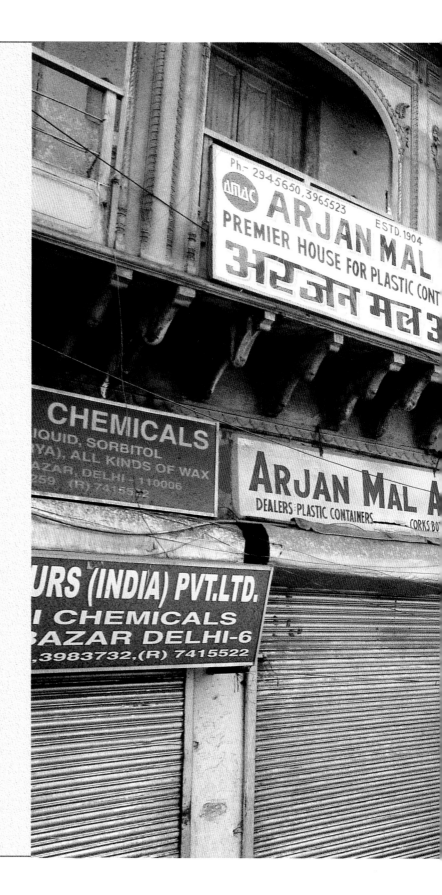

enclosed by the great walls. The walled areas are, in fact, only the hub of the urban complex and the extensions of the city house a good deal of economic and social life. These institutions and buildings can easily be construed as the thread that holds together the cultural, social and economic life of Shahjahanabad. However, with changing times and a modern work culture, buildings have undergone a sea change in their functional values.

Gone are the days of imperial *karkhanahs* or workshops, when the ruling elite lived off the labour of others, who were regarded as working solely for the gratification of the rulers. During the Mughal period, there were merchants and traders on the one hand, and moneylenders or *sahukars* on the other. Along with these came other associations and guilds that took care of education and other social needs. With the passage of time, social awareness led to the foundation of many such institutions. The city blended within its parameters, both a lavish social life and a hectic business culture.

The workplaces of Shahjahanabad are the former residences of some of the nobles. Today, they are used as offices and institutions as well as for commercial purposes. The foresight of those who built these large, spacious buildings is as surprising as it is commendable.

Shahjahanabad is home to innumerable educational institutions, inns, banks, offices, hospitals et al. The substructure of modern society—all the institutions that supply society with its needs and wants—sits squarely in glorious ancient buildings. This part of the world boasts of the first girls' school as well as the first hotel in the whole city. The Old Delhi Railway Station, perhaps the most well-known landmark of the area, came into existence a hundred and forty years ago. This is just the tip of the iceberg. Some of the most prized possessions of the city are the envy of the whole world. From the wealthy and powerful to the common man, everyone has something to do with the city. Here, work is not just a ritual but is tied inextricably to the very sense of 'being'.

The inhabitants of Shahjahanabad had a deep love for singers and musicians, and the memories of those old cultural icons can be traced through these places. The deafening buzz of business in this area today, has very nearly drowned the sound of enchanting music and the tinkle of ankle bells. Banks, madrasas and

religious institutions vie for the scarce space available in Shahjahanabad.

The communities living here must indeed be praised for keeping their surroundings culturally alive despite changing times. The upper class had the sensitivity to devote time and money for charitable causes not just for their name and fame, but for spiritual satisfaction. In Shahjahanabad, charity and charitable people have not faded away: in many places of interest, portraits, pictures and documents still reflect what they have contributed to society.

The contributions of British missionaries and individuals are also worth cherishing. They did much for social causes such as education and health, and their help led to better services for the masses to a considerable extent.

It is said that Shahjahanabad was originally designed to house a population of 70,000. Yet, because of its growing prosperity it had nearly 2,50,000 inhabitants in Aurangzeb's reign. By the time the British finished wreaking vengeance in the aftermath of the 1857 Mutiny, the city was left with approximately the population it was designed for: 60,000. Since then, the capacity to produce something new and charming has been on a decline. What is left behind is chaos and a variety of unplanned activities. The result is a haphazard mélange of a creative past and a mundane present.

Add to this the unchecked march of modern materialism and the gradual change of values that this has brought about. Today, most residents live in the hope of material gain and not so much for the fulfilment of any creative urge. The growing apathy towards preserving one's heritage, which has led to the loss of many beautiful buildings, is a symptom of the times. In fact, the working conditions in Shahjahanabad are not good at all. However, the various institutions, schools and dharmashalas are interwoven so finely into the social fabric that they offer a balancing factor to the city: a framework of the traditional values that seem to have been built into them.

Shahjahanabad continues to throb with life and humanitarian values, the existence of a bond of brotherhood binding the different communities together. This harmony, however, is just as fragile today as the old buildings of the city. It needs to be consciously sustained and preserved since burgeoning economic activity is affecting the cultural rhythm of the city.

Hotel Oberoi Maidens

LOCATION: Shamnath Marg, Civil Lines.

SIGNIFICANCE: Mr Maiden built this hotel in 1900. It was among the first hotels to be built in the city.

EXPLICATION: The three-storeyed building has a small projecting porch leading to the lobby and the veranda. The large wooden and glass windows and doors between the columns of the ground floor and the high ceilings are commendable features of this gracious hotel.

Those who checked in

Edward Lutyens, the architect of Rashtrapati Bhavan, lived here and it was here that a grand ball was organized in honour of the 27-year-old Edward, Prince of Wales.

Indraprastha College

LOCATION: Shamnath Marg, Civil Lines.

SIGNIFICANCE: Indraprastha College for Women was founded in 1924. Its first principal Leonara G. Miner was an Australian. The present premises of the college were the office-cum-residence of the British Commander-in-Chief. It is also referred to as Alipore House and was built in 1912. The college was formally inaugurated on 7 February 1939.

EXPLICATION: The single-storeyed building has a facade marked by a series of semi-circular arches supported on circular columns. The front courtyard has royal palm trees and a fountain.

Famous visitors

The college is the oldest women's college. Many famous personalities, such as the Late Indira Gandhi, Annie Besant and Prime Minister Atal Bihari Vajpayee have paid it a visit.

Bagh Deewar Dharamshala

LOCATION: 1, Bagh Deewar, Fatehpuri.

SIGNIFICANCE: The building with a grand late Mughal-style facade made of buff-coloured sandstone was constructed in the late nineteenth century.

EXPLICATION: Now commercialized, it has an exquisitely carved facade with floral motifs in the stone *chattris* on the corners and intricate engravings at the opening. The central courtyard is surrounded by shops. Some superb craftsmanship can be seen in its sandstone brackets and the arch-vaulted roofs.

Queen Mary's School

LOCATION: Sarai Phoos, Tis Hazari.

SIGNIFICANCE: Helen Jerwood, an Englishwoman, established the school in 1912. The main objective was to educate women at a time when education for women was not encouraged.

EXPLICATION: Built around a central courtyard in the same year as its establishment, the building has sandstone framing for arches and battlements over the entrance. Stately high ceilings and colonial elements mark the inner rooms. Local stone has been used in the construction of the original school building and school auditorium. The alumni include such illustrious personalities as Anita Desai, Begum Abida Ahmed and Sucheta Kripalani.

General Post Office (GPO)

LOCATION: Lothian Road, near the Railway Bridge, Kashmere Gate.

SIGNIFICANCE: The General Post Office is counted among the biggest post offices in Asia and was established in 1885.

EXPLICATION: This classic, colonial double-storeyed building has five arched bays marked by semi-circular arched gateways on the ground floor. Circular pillars and elaborate mouldings are present over the doorway on the ground floor.

The nerve centre of the raj

The General Post Office (GPO) has been awarded for its services and excellence many times by the postal department. The GPO held a strategic position during the British period, being the centre of its communications system.

Cambridge Brotherhood Society

LOCATION: 7, Court Lane, adjacent to the Lieutenant Governor's Office, Civil Lines.

SIGNIFICANCE: The Cambridge Brotherhood began its work in Delhi in 1877 and was responsible for founding the prestigious St. Stephen's College. The Society had a number of brilliant scholars associated with it.

EXPLICATION: The Delhi quartzite stone building has a porch that leads to a deep veranda with an arcade. Semi-circular arches span the roof of the chapel at the rear. There is an attractive enclosed courtyard. The Delhi Brotherhood Society, formerly known as Cambridge Brotherhood Society, comes under the Church of North India (CNI). It undertakes various small projects in the field of social welfare.

Madarsa Amima Islamia Arabia

LOCATION: Bara Bazaar, Kashmere Gate.

SIGNIFICANCE: This well-maintained madrasa came up in Sunehri Mosque, Chandni Chowk, in 1897.

EXPLICATION: There is a grand carved Mughal-style entrance gateway, and the central arch has small cusped arched windows on either side. There is an entrance vestibule that leads to a large court with a tank in the centre and an arched arcade on all four sides with a mosque on one side. The mosque, named the Panipatian Masjid, is said to be at least eight hundred years old. The madrasa is made of beautiful sandstone and *lakhori* bricks. It caters to the education of children, and students from Mewat, Bihar and Kashmir come especially to study here.

Old St. Stephen's College

LOCATION: Zorawar Singh Marg, opposite St. James Church, Kashmere Gate.

SIGNIFICANCE: Designed by Samuel Swinton Jacob, this building came into existence in 1890.

EXPLICATION: The two-storeyed building has magnificent engravings on sandstone on its facade and a majestic porch. Arched colonnades and semi-octagonal turrets with a domed pavilion lend a stately appeal to the building. It was part of the old campus of St. Stephen's College.

To the glory of god

There is a plaque at the entrance to the office that states: To the glory of God and for the advancement of sound learning and religious education, St. Stephen's College, Delhi. Sir Charles A. Elliot, K.E.S.I, laid the foundation stone on Friday, 11 April 1890. The building presently houses the office of the Election Commission, Government of the National Capital Territory (NCT) of Delhi.

Haveli Sultan Singh (NCC Office)

LOCATION: Kashmere Gate Market, Chabi Ganj, Kashmere Gate.

SIGNIFICANCE: Built in the 1890s this building is popularly known as Sultan Singh's residence. Lala Sultan Singh was a famous moneylender and banker of his time and played an important role in the establishment of the Indraprastha Hindu Kanya Vidyalaya, behind Jama Masjid. His grandson, General Virendra Singh, was one of the founders of the National Cadet Corps (NCC).

EXPLICATION: Constructed of Delhi quartzite stone, the entrance to the house is through an upper floor reached by a flight of fourteen stairs. *Jharokha*-like openings and exquisite ceramic tile work adorn the facade. Behind the front veranda, there is a large hall with a fireplace; a corridor separates it from rooms on the side. The relief work on the walls, the projecting balcony and on the ceilings is extremely decorative.

Bachchon ka Ghar

LOCATION: Opposite H.M.D.A.V. School, Daryaganj.

SIGNIFICANCE: Established in 1891 in Kamra Bangash by Moidul Islam, the institution was shifted to this building in 1940. The former President of India, the late Dr Zakir Hussain, christened it Bachchon Ka Ghar. The institution helps destitute children.

EXPLICATION: The entrance to the building is through a beautiful semi-circular arched entrance with decorative platforms on both sides. The exquisite screen work and four minarets are worth seeing. The rooms are large and have high ceilings. Important personalities such as Hakim Ajmal Khan and former Presidents Dr Rajendra Prasad, Dr Zakir Hussain, Janab Fakhruddin Ali Ahmed and Giani Zail Singh have been associated with this institution.

Anglo-Arabic Public School

LOCATION: Ajmeri Gate.

SIGNIFICANCE: Built in the early eighteenth century, this Mughal building has been awarded the Delhi Development Authority (DDA) Urban Heritage Award for its importance as a centre of learning.

EXPLICATION: This double-storeyed building is constructed around a courtyard with *jharokhas* on the inner side of the gateway. The gateway has a domed roof, minarets and battlements. Decorative floral patterns and red sandstone feature in the windows, in the *jaali* work and in the doorways. It was a school where Arabic and traditional sciences were taught in Persian, the language of the Mughal court.

From madrasa to college

In 1824, the old madrasa was repaired and renamed Delhi College. In the 1840s, it became the centre of a rich cultural flowering known as the Delhi Renaissance. Cultural evenings were held here. All this came to an end with the 1857 Mutiny. The Britishers occupied the school and it was never able to regain its prestige.

Girdharilal School

LOCATION: 5, Bagh Deewar, Chandni Chowk.

SIGNIFICANCE: Built in the late nineteenth century.

EXPLICATION: This mansion has an ornamental sandstone entrance leading to a large courtyard. The facade has fine floral carvings and designs displaying superb craftsmanship. The semi-circular arched entrances and a window on the first floor make the building rather attractive. There is a temple inside the building while the rest of the area functions as a school.

Entrusted to the seths

The building is part of the Seth Gopal Das Trust. There is a portrait in one of the rooms that shows Englishmen and Indian businessmen together. It is believed that the Indians in the portrait belong to the Seth Gopal Das family.

Indraprastha Hindu Kanya Vidyalaya

LOCATION: Behind Jama Masjid, Shahjahanabad.

SIGNIFICANCE: Established in 1904 by Seth Jugal Kishore. Leonora G. Miner, an Australian, was the first principal. Housed in a haveli dating back to 1857 and built on the central courtyard plan, the school fuses Hindu and Muslim architecture. Known as Bhajan Bhavan, it was dedicated in 1907 to the cause of education of women.

EXPLICATION: It has two main entrances. The one on the Jama Masjid side represents Islamic architecture with intricate floral carvings and pointed semi-circular arched entrances. The other on Chippiwara Street represents Hindu deities, birds and auspicious symbols in a traditional style. The main hall in the haveli has a decorative fireplace, arched niches and a sword. An imperial crown is artistically represented on the wall. Stained glass and a functional well lend an old-world charm to the structure.

A roll call of famous students

The hall was a centre of gathering of people from different faiths. It had beautiful *jharokhas*, now closed, from where the ladies of the royal family could take a look at the activities taking place in the hall. Ms Kamla Nehru, Dr Kapila Vatsyayan, Dr Sharan Rani Backliwal and Ms Sarla Sharma studied in this school. Famous dignitaries in the pre-Independence period who visited the school included Pandit Jawaharlal Nehru, Dr Annie Besant, Sarojini Naidu and Gurudev Rabindranath Tagore.

Old Delhi Railway Station

LOCATION: S.P. Mukherjee Marg, Shahjahanabad.

SIGNIFICANCE: Built by Sir Ronald MacDonald Stephenson of the East India Company in 1864, it is among the earliest railway stations the British constructed in India.

EXPLICATION: The two-storeyed building has several Gothic features with deep verandas on both floors. Semi-octagonal turrets rise from the corners of the building. There are nineteen platforms for the broad gauge and three for the metre gauge.

200 trains and 200,000 people

The station is listed among the ten important railway stations of India and handles around 200 trains daily. It was initially planned for just 10,000 people. Now, it caters everyday to the needs of more than 200,000 people!

Shri Marwari Aushadhalaya

LOCATION: 2766, Chatta Pratap Singh, Kinari Bazaar, Chandni Chowk.

SIGNIFICANCE: Built in the late nineteenth century with the present *Aushadhalaya* (dispensary) opening in 1932. The *Aushadhalaya* has a long history of association with personalities such as Shri Morarji Desai, Babu Jagjiwan Ram, Shri Hans Raj Gupta and Shri Kedarnath Moda. It comes under the Shri Marwari Trust.

EXPLICATION: Built on the central courtyard plan, it has a semi-circular arched entrance built of stone with exquisite carvings on the doorways. The facade of the building is made of sandstone with mouldings and Hindu religious figurines on the front. The designs on the ceramic tiles, the arched niches with mirror work and screen work are some of the other notable features.

Shri Marwari Public Library

LOCATION: Above Haldiram Sweets, Main Road, Chandni Chowk.
SIGNIFICANCE: The late Seth Kedarnath Goenka established it in 1915.
The library played an important role in the struggle for Independence,
when it was a meeting point for the freedom fighters and leaders who
created an awareness about the freedom struggle.
EXPLICATION: Functioning from the first floor, the library reflects a
fascinating mix of colonial and classical architectural styles. It has semi-
circular arched windows and iron pillars. With a collection of three
thousand rare Hindi and Urdu books, it has been awarded the Delhi
Development Authority (DDA) Urban Heritage Award.

Valuable manuscripts

Great leaders and freedom
fighters such as Bal
Gangadhar Tilak, Bal Krishna
Gokhale and Pandit Madan
Mohan Malviya visited the
library. Their handwritten
manuscripts are still the pride
of the library.

State Bank of India Building

LOCATION: Main Road, Chandni Chowk.

SIGNIFICANCE: Established in 1861 as Delhi and London Bank, the Delhi branch of the Bank of Bengal was shifted to this location in 1923.

EXPLICATION: This three-storeyed building has very high ceilings on each floor. Two large gateposts are typical of colonial architecture. Corinthian pillars with floral carvings and *jaali* openings are other notable features.

The SBI story

The building in the heart of Old Delhi's bustling business centre, which once housed the court of English rulers, was acquired by the Delhi Bank in 1847. It was here that the freedom fighters assassinated George Beresford, an agent of the bank, his wife and five daughters in 1857. The Imperial Bank of India (predecessor of the SBI) later acquired the building. The Reserve Bank of India operated from here. Enriched with Corinthian pillars, a balustraded terrace, arched doorways, spiral iron staircases, old English lifts and printed glass windows, the building epitomizes the elegance of European architecture. The imposing Palladian edifice dominates the business stretch of Chandni Chowk even to this day.

Allahabad Bank Building

LOCATION: 4940, Chandni Chowk, beyond Town Hall.

SIGNIFICANCE: Built in the 1930s, this three-storeyed building, once the residence of a nobleman, has a decorative facade with arches on it.

EXPLICATION: Today the ground floor houses several shops while the upper two floors are in their original state. The building exhibits colonial features in the capitals of the circular plasters and the lattice screen on the front.

St. Stephen's Community Centre

LOCATION: 4, Rajpur Road, Civil Lines.

SIGNIFICANCE: Built in 1909, this colonial building is now used for community services. It has a chapel and is related to St. Stephen's Hospital that was established in 1908 in Chandni Chowk.

EXPLICATION: This single-storeyed building has an arcaded veranda with semi-circular arches. The chapel inside has old stained glass windows and a memorial plaque which enumerates the name of the wardens since 1896. Built of Delhi quartzite stone, the building has small semi-circular arched windows.

The Town Hall is the venue for
many debates and discussions.

Town Hall

LOCATION: Main Road, Chandni Chowk.

SIGNIFICANCE: This is the Office of the Municipal Commissioner of
Delhi and was built on the site of Begum Ki Sarai and Bagh (the present
Company Bagh) in 1860-64 according to the Victoria plan. It was among
the first British buildings to be built in Shahjahanabad after the 1857
Mutiny.

EXPLICATION: An impressive double-storeyed building with arched
openings, it is built around a courtyard. The Town Hall has arched
window openings, parapets, Corinthian capitals, mouldings and a
beautiful porch.

When statues were switched

Known as Lawrence Institute and later as Institute Building, the Town
Hall has a significant history. The Municipal Corporation of Delhi
purchased it after much effort in 1866. To remove the last traces of a
colonial past, the statue of Swami Shradhanand replaced that of Queen
Victoria in front of the Town Hall. The famous Ghanta Ghar stood nearby.
On the main road, the statue of Swami Shradhanand has a plaque that
mentions the special assembly of the Congress, the Rowlett Act of
1929, and a historic procession.

Mahavir Jain Bhawan

LOCATION: 1417. Main Road, Chandni Chowk.

SIGNIFICANCE: Built in 1905 by Lala Gokul Chand Nahar, a prominent social worker, the Bhawan, popularly known as Baradari, has its own identity and significance among the Jain community. Jain sadhus and *sadhvis* perform religious activities in the presence of thousands of devotees of all sects who visit the Bhawan. Among other religious festivals, Mahavira Nirvana Diwas is celebrated here annually the day after Diwali.

EXPLICATION: The double-storeyed building with mouldings, flower motifs on parapets and other sandstone details has a lecture hall and a very old library on the first floor. The library's antiquities contain a visitor's book, with the signatures of many eminent leaders belonging to the National Freedom Movement. Ancient and religious texts on Jainism such as *Bhagwata Sutra*, *Uttradhyana Sutra* and *Chandrapragyapati Sutra* are also present in the Bhawan's collection.

Hardayal Municipal Library

LOCATION: Hardayal Municipal Library, Gandhi Maidan, Delhi.

SIGNIFICANCE : Established in 1916 the Hardayal Municipal Library is Delhi's oldest library. On December 12, 1912 a bomb was hurled at Lord Hardinge by a group of freedom fighters, led by Lala Hardayal, while he was passing through Chandni Chowk in a procession on an elephant. To mark Lord Hardinge's escape, a committee was delegated to construct a building of architectural merit under the presidentship of Rai Bahadur Lala Sheo Prasad.

EXPLICATION: In the nineteenth century, many English officers came to India with a large selection of books with them. On their return to England these books were often abandoned and found a home in the reading club. The collection became the basis of the Public Library known as the Institute Library in the Town Hall. The present building is built around a central double height room with a plaque on the entrance explaining the reasons for its foundation. In 1972, it was renamed after Lala Hardayal. It is also known as the Hardinge Library. The library has a collection of more than 170,000 books in Hindi, English, Urdu, Arabic, Persian and Sanskrit.

Heritage Walks: Passages to history

Heritage Walk – 1

Walk Chandni Chowk
Main Road via Red Fort to Fatehpuri Mosque'

Walk – II

Jama Masjid and Around

Walk – III

Turkman Gate and Masjid Hauz Qazi Chowk

Walk – IV

Kashmere Gate and Around

Walk – V

Ajmeri Gate

For visiting monument 6 and 7 rickshaw is recommended from the last monument.

Walk – VI

Civil Lines

Walk – VII

Delhi Gate

Index

Seen from the top of the Gadodia Market Khari Baoli adjacent to the Fatehpuri Masjid, the Red Fort (foreground) and the Jama Masjid (far right).

Aerial View of Chandni Chowk

Bibliography

1. Asher, C.B., Architecture of Mughal India, Cambridge, 1992.
2. Bernier Francoise, Travels in the Mogul Empire 1656-68, edited by Archibald Constable, translated by Irving Brock, S. Chand & Co, Reprinted edition, 1972.
3. Blake Stephen P., Shahjahanabad The Sovereign City in Mughal India 1634-1739, Oxford University Press, Delhi, 1993.
4. Carr Stephen, The Archaeology and Monumental Remains of Delhi, Calcutta, 1876.
5. Dayal Maheshwar, Rediscovering Delhi: The Story of Shahjahanabad, 2nd edition, S. Chand & Co. Ltd., Delhi, 1982.
6. Delhi, INTACH Chapter—Delhi: The Built Heritage A Listing.
7. Fanshawe, H.C., Delhi: Past and Present, Delhi, 1902, Aryan Books International, New Delhi, reprinted 1979.
8. Frykenberg, R.E., Delhi through Images: Essays in Urban History, Culture and Society, Oxford University Press, Delhi, 1986.
9. Gupta Narayani, Delhi between Two Empires 1803-1931, Oxford University Press, Delhi, 1999.
10. Issar, T.P., Diwan-e-Ghalib, T. P. Issar, Bangalore, 1999.
11. Kaul, H.K., ed., Historic Delhi: An Anthology, Oxford University Press, Delhi, 1985.
12. Koch Ebba, Mughal Architecture: An Outline, Munich, 1999.
13. Nicholson Louise, The Red Fort, Delhi, Tauris Parke Books, London, 1989.
14. Rehman Aziz-ur, History of Jama Masjid and Interpretation of Muslim Devotions, Publications India, New Delhi, 1987.
15. Sharma, Y.D., Delhi and its Neighbourhood, 2nd edition, Archaeological Survey of India, Delhi, 1974.
16. Spear Percival, A History of Delhi under the late Mughals, D.K. Publishers, New Delhi, 1995.
17. Spear Percival, 'Twilight of the Mughuls', Studies in late Mughul Delhi, Cambridge University Press, 1951.
18. Varma, P. K., Shankar, S., Havelis of Old Delhi, Spantech Publishers, England and Bookwise (India) Pvt. Ltd, 1992, reprint 1999.
19. Zafar Hassan Maulvi, 'Monuments of Delhi,' Lasting Splendour of Great Mughals and Others, Vol. I, Aryan Books International, New Delhi, 1997.